"Guiding Change Journeys is a masterful fusion of Eastern a[nd]
science, and mythology presented with great insight, clari[ty]
full of new ideas, tools, and practical applications that are
gize and reorient your thinking and approach to organizati[ons]
    —Robert J. Marshak, Ph.D.
        organizational consultant and author of
        "Lewin Meets Confucius: A Re-View of the OD Model of Change"

"Rebecca Chan Allen has created an exciting road map for a journey of change.
Her landscape is complete with dragons, deep pits, and pathfinders to stimulate both the guide and the process of organization change."
    —T. Don Stacy
        corporate director, Noble Affiliates, Hydril Co., AEC Ltd., and Agrium,
        former chair of Amoco Canada and Amoco Eurasia

"The publication of *Guiding Change Journeys* is a reason for celebration for all of
us involved with change in organizations. Rebecca Chan Allen's approach
works for organizations and individuals and is taking hold as a model for
leading change that addresses what is going on during the change process for
our organizations and ourselves. *Guiding Change Journeys* is thoughtfully written with real-life lessons and case studies that show how to use the book's
innovative methodologies. I recommend this book to everyone involved in the
journey of change."
    —Dr. Robert I. Tobin
        professor, Faculty of Business and Commerce, Keio University, Tokyo, Japan

"Rebecca Chan Allen has the unique qualifications of award-winning change
practitioner, multicultural teacher, cancer survivor, and global citizen to both
tell stories about transformation and to teach us the archetypal path to community. Change practitioners daunted by complex projects will find this book
brimming with useful tools to bring clarity and direct their efforts toward
success."
    —Dr. Holly Benkert
        president, Madison Consulting

"By introducing a unique approach (Archetypal Change Journey), the author
contributes to the dialogue on organization transformation and provides practical examples through matrices, mandalas, and metaphors. She took me into
new territories by way of triangulating the new sciences, mythology, and
diverse cultural traditions to enmesh universal themes in a one-world multicultural community perspective. Her thought-provoking theory and creative
practices of change 'jump' off the pages into the real world of work and personal 'discovery' that I plan to use and share."
    —Argentine Saunders Craig, Ph.D.
        faculty emeritus, The Fielding Institute, Santa Barbara, California

"Illuminates both the theoretical and practical side of today's greatest organizational issue and gives senior leaders the means to play full, rich, transforming roles in organization change."

—Layton S. Fisher
former manager of organization effectiveness,
Esso Resources Canada Limited

"This book is a rare gift from a successful international organization development consultant in which Dr. Chan Allen shares personal, organizational, and cultural epiphanies. Change agents are presented theory and techniques as they are challenged to confront their own journey as well as the journey of the organizations with which they work."

—Dr. Barbara P. Mink
faculty, The Fielding Institute, Santa Barbara, California

"In *Guiding Change Journeys,* Dr. Chan Allen capitalizes on the perspectives gained from diversity to describe eight synergistic practices that 'awaken the creative energy in organizations and people.' This innovative methodology will be invaluable to change agents and organizational leaders in deepening their purpose, clarity, and commitment and in moving individuals and organizations forward."

—Patricia Dawson, MD, Ph.D.
author of *Forged by the Knife: The Experience of Surgical
Residency from the Perspective of a Woman of Color*

"*Guiding Change Journeys* has elegance and pacing that by itself is a guide to the often frantic change efforts of Western consultants. Rebecca Chan Allen has laid out a process for mapping journeys to take a person, an organization, or a community into a more harmonious and effective place, using taoist wisdom to create resonance in Western settings. The work is expansive, opening us to new, but ancient, views while aiding us with practical tools and examples of successful change efforts. It is a book to sit with, absorb, and reflect upon. It can teach us all new ways of making changes that make a difference."

—Will McWhinney
president, Enthusion, Inc., author of *Paths of Change:
Strategic Choices for Organizations and Society*

Practicing Organization Development

**The Change Agent Series
for Groups and Organizations**

MISSION STATEMENT

The books in this series are intended to be cutting-edge, state-of-the-art, and innovative approaches to participative change in organizational settings. They are written for, and written by, organization development (OD) practitioners interested in new approaches to facilitating participative change. They are geared to providing both theory and advice on practical application.

SERIES EDITORS

**William J. Rothwell
Roland Sullivan
Kristine Quade**

EDITORIAL BOARD

**David Bradford
W. Warner Burke
Edith Whitfield Seashore
Robert Tannenbaum
Christopher G. Worley
Shaolin Zhang**

Guiding
Change
Journeys

To Janet,
Thank you for your
care and support.
May you enjoy
fulfillment in all your
journeys.

With love,
Rebecca.
Sept 21, 2001

Guiding Change Journeys

A Synergistic Approach to Organization Transformation

Rebecca Chan Allen
Foreword by Richard Beckhard

JOSSEY-BASS/PFEIFFER
A Wiley Company
www.pfeiffer.com

Practicing
Organization
Development

Published by

JOSSEY-BASS/PFEIFFER
A Wiley Company
989 Market Street
San Francisco, CA 94103-1741
415.433.1740; Fax 415.433.0499
800.274.4434; Fax 800.569.0443

www.pfeiffer.com

Jossey-Bass/Pfeiffer is a registered trademark of Jossey-Bass Inc., A Wiley Company.

ISBN: 0-7879-5711-9

Library of Congress Cataloging-in-Publication Data

Allen, Rebecca Chan, 1950-
  Guiding change journeys : a synergistic approach to
organization transformation / Rebecca Chan Allen.
      p. cm. — (The practicing organization development
series)
Includes bibliographical references and index.
  ISBN 0-7879-5711-9
  1. Organizational change—Handbooks, manuals, etc. I. Title.
II. Series.
  HD58.8 .A6777 2002
  658.4'06—dc21

2001002024

Printed in the United States of America.

We at Jossey-Bass strive to use the most environmentally sensitive paper stocks available to us. Our publications are printed on acid-free recycled stock whenever possible, and our paper always meets or exceeds minimum GPO and EPA requirements.

Jossey-Bass/Pfeiffer is a registered trademark of Jossey-Bass Inc., A Wiley Company.

Acquiring Editor: Matthew Holt
Director of Development: Kathleen Dolan Davies
Developmental Editor: Susan Rachmeler
Editor: Rebecca Taff

Senior Production Editor: Dawn Kilgore
Manufacturing Supervisor: Becky Carreño
Interior and Cover Design: Bruce Lundquist
Illustrations: Richard Sheppard

Printing 10 9 8 7 6 5 4 3 2 1

Contents

List of Tables, Figures, and Exhibits

Foreword
to the Series

ON **1967,** Warren Bennis, Ed Schein, and I were faculty members of the Sloan School of Management at MIT. We decided to produce a series of paperback books that collectively would describe the state of the field of organization development (OD). Organization development as a field had been named by myself and several others from our pioneer change effort at General Mills in Minneapolis, Minnesota, some ten years earlier.

Today I define OD as "a systemic and systematic change effort, using behavioral science knowledge and skill, to transform the organization to a new state."

In any case, several books and many articles had been written, but there was no consensus on whether OD was a field of practice, an area of study, or a profession. We had not even established OD as a theory or even as a practice.

We decided that there was a need for something that would describe the state of OD. Our intention was to each write a book and also to recruit three other authors. After some searching, we found a young editor who had just joined the small publishing house of Addison-Wesley. We made contact, and the series was born. Our audience was to be human resource professionals who spent their time consulting with managers in their development through various small-group activities, such as team building. More than thirty books have been published in that series, and the series has had a life of its own. We just celebrated its thirtieth anniversary.

At last year's National OD Network Conference, I said that it was time for the OD profession to change and transform itself. Is that not what we change agents tell our clients to do? This new Jossey-Bass/Pfeiffer series will do just that. It can be seen as:

- A documentation of the re-invention of OD;

- An effort that will take us to the next level; and

- A practical effort to transfer to the world the theory and practice of leading-edge practitioners and theorists.

The books in this new series will thus prove to be valuable resources for change agents to keep current with the new and leading-edge ideas and practices.

May this very exciting change agent series be most creative and innovative. May it give our field a renewed burst of energy and awareness.

Richard Beckhard
Written on Labor Day weekend 1999 from my summer cabin near Bethel, Maine

Introduction
to the Series

"We must become the change we want to see."

—*Mahatma Gandhi*

"We live in a moment of history where change is so speeded up that we begin to see the present only when it is already disappearing."

—*R. D. Laing*

WE CAN EXPECT MORE CHANGE to occur in our lifetimes than has occurred since the beginning of civilization over ten thousand years ago. *Practicing Organization Development: The Change Agent Series for Groups and Organizations* is a new series of books being launched to help those who must cope with or create change in organizational settings. That includes almost everyone.

The Current State of Organization Development

Our view of OD in this series is an optimistic one. We believe that OD is gaining favor as decision makers realize that a balance *must* be struck between the drivers of change and the people involved in it and affected by it. Although OD does have its disadvantages at a time characterized by quantum leap change, it remains preferable to such alternative approaches to change as coercion, persuasion, leadership change, and debate.[1] Organization development practitioners are reinventing their approaches, based on certain foundational roots of the field, in combination with emerging principles to ensure that OD will increasingly be recognized as a viable, important, and inherently participative approach to help people in organizations facilitate, anticipate, and manage change.

A Brief History of the Genesis of the OD Series

A few years ago, and as a direct result of the success of _Practicing Organization Development: A Guide for Practitioners_ by Rothwell, Sullivan, and McLean, the publisher—feeling that OD was experiencing a rebirth of interest in the United States and in other nations—wanted to launch a new OD series. The goal of this new series was not to replace, or even compete directly with, the well-established Addison-Wesley OD Series (edited by Edgar Schein). Instead, as the editors saw it, this series would provide a means by which the most promising authors in OD whose voices had not previously been heard could share their ideas. The publisher enlisted the support of Bill Rothwell, Roland Sullivan, and Kristine Quade to turn the dream of a series into a reality.

This series was long in the making. After sharing many discussions with the publisher and circulating among themselves several draft descriptions of the series editorial guidelines, the editors were guests of Bob Tannenbaum, one of the field's founders, in Carmel, California, in February 1999 to discuss the series with a group of well-known OD practitioners interested in authoring books. Several especially supportive publisher representatives, including Matt Holt and Josh Blatter, were also present at that weekend-long meeting. It was an opportunity for diverse OD practitioners, representing many philosophical viewpoints, to come together to share their vision for a new book series. In a sense, this series represents an OD intervention in the OD field in that it is geared to bringing change to the field most closely associated with change management and facilitation.

---

[1]W. Rothwell, R. Sullivan, & G. McLean. (1995). Introduction (pp. 3–46). In W. Rothwell, R. Sullivan, & G. McLean, _Practicing Organization Development: A Guide for Consultants._ San Francisco, CA: Jossey-Bass/ Pfeiffer.

What Distinguishes the Books in this Series

The books in this series are meant to be cutting-edge and state-of-the-art in their approach to OD. The goal of the series is to provide an outlet for proven authorities in OD who have not put their ideas into print or for up-and-coming writers in OD who have new, sometimes unorthodox, approaches that are stimulating and exciting. Some of the books in this series describe inspirational concepts that can lead to actionable change and purvey ideas so new that they are not fully developed.

Unique to this series is the cutting-edge emphasis, the immediate applicability, and the ease of transferability of the concepts. The aim of this series is nothing less than to reinvent, re-energize, and reinvigorate OD. In each book, we have also recommended that the author(s) provide:

- A research base of some kind, meaning new information derived from practice and/or systematic investigation and

- Practical tools, worksheets, case studies and other ready-to-go approaches that help the authors drag "theory" to "practice" to make these new, cutting-edge approaches more concrete.

Subject Matter That Will (and Will Not) Be Covered

The books in this series are varied in their approach, but they are united by their focus. All share an emphasis on organization development (OD). Hence, books in this series are about participative change efforts. They are not about such other popular topics as leadership, management development, consulting, group dynamics—unless those topics are treated in new, cutting-edge ways and are geared to OD practitioners.

This Book

As the transformation of our planet gathers momentum, change leaders and facilitators are guiding organizations through uncharted territory. In *Guiding Change Journeys*, Rebecca Chan Allen takes you on an exhilarating change odyssey of personal and organization transformation. She integrates ideas and practices from mythology, new science, wisdom traditions, and Eastern and Western change perspectives to create a practical synergistic approach to organization change. She tells stories of change leaders and facilitators, confronted by business volatility and burgeoning organization diversity, who use scientific insights and timeless change techniques to transform impasse into innovation and conflicts into creativity. The perspectives and tools in this book can help you and your organization embrace the unknown and venture into new territory with clarity and confidence.

Series Website

For further information and resources about the books in this series and about the current and future practice of organization development, we encourage readers to visit the series website at *www.PracticingOD.Pfeiffer.com.*

William J. Rothwell
University Park, PA

Roland Sullivan
Deephaven, MN

Kristine Quade
Minnetonka, MN

Statement
of the Board

OT IS OUR PLEASURE TO PARTICIPATE in and influence the start up of *Practicing Organization Development: The Change Agent Series for Groups and Organizations.* The purpose of the series is to stimulate the profession and influence how OD is defined and practiced. This statement is intended to set the context for the series by addressing three important questions: (1) What is OD? (2) Is the OD profession at a crossroads? and (3) What is the purpose of this series?

What Is Organization Development?

We offer the following definition of OD to stimulate debate:

> Organization development is a system-wide and values-based collaborative process of applying behavioral science knowledge to the adaptive development, improvement, and reinforcement of such organizational features as the strategies, structures, processes, people, and cultures that lead to organization effectiveness.

The definition suggests that OD can be understood in terms of its several foci:

First, *OD is a system-wide process.* It works with whole systems. In the past, the bias has been toward working at the individual and group levels. More recently, the focus has shifted to organizations and multi-organization systems. We support that trend in general but honor and acknowledge the fact that the traditional focus on smaller systems is both legitimate and necessary.

Second, *OD is values-based.* Traditionally, OD has attempted to distinguish itself from other forms of planned change and applied behavioral science by promoting a set of humanistic values and by emphasizing the importance of personal growth as a key to its practice. Today, that focus is blurred and there is much debate about the value base underlying the practice of OD. We support a more formal and direct conversation about what these values are and how the field is related to them.

Third, *OD is collaborative.* Our first value commitment as OD practitioners is to bring about an inclusive, diverse workforce with a focus of integrating differences into a world-wide culture mentality.

Fourth, *OD is based on behavioral science knowledge.* Organization development should incorporate and apply knowledge from sociology, psychology, anthropology, technology, and economics toward the end of making systems more effective. We support the continued emphasis in OD on behavioral science knowledge and believe that OD practitioners should be widely read and comfortable with several of the disciplines.

Fifth, *OD is concerned with the adaptive development, improvement, and reinforcement of strategies, structures, processes, people, culture, and other features of organizational life.* This statement not only describes the organizational elements that are the target of change, but also describes the process by which effectiveness is increased. That is, OD works in a variety of areas, and it is focused on improving these areas. We believe that such a statement of process and content strongly implies that a key feature of OD is the transference of knowledge and skill to the system so that it is more able to handle and manage change in the future.

Sixth and finally, *OD is about improving organization effectiveness.* It is not just about making people happy; it is also concerned with meeting financial goals, improving productivity, and addressing stakeholder satisfaction. We believe that OD's future is closely tied to the incorporation of this value in its purpose and the demonstration of this objective in its practice.

Is the OD Profession at a Crossroads?

For years, OD professionals have said that OD is at a crossroads. From our perspective at the beginning of the new millennium, the field of organization development can be characterized by the following statements:

1. Practitioners today are torn. The professional organizations representing OD practitioners, including the OD Network, the OD Institute, the International OD Association, and the Academy of Management's OD and Change Division, are experiencing tremendous uncertainties in their purposes, practices, and relationships.

2. There are increasing calls for regulation/certification.

3. Many respected practitioners have suggested that people who profess to manage change are behind those who are creating it. Organization development practitioners should lead through influence rather than follow the lead of those who are sometimes coercive in their approach to change.

4. The field is defined by techniques.

5. The values that guide the field are unclear and ill-defined.

6. Too many people are practicing OD without any training in the field.

7. Practitioners are having difficulty figuring out how to market their services.

The situation suggests the following provocative questions:

- How can OD practitioners help formulate strategy, shape the strategy development process, contribute to the content of strategy, and drive how strategy will be implemented?

- How can OD practitioners encourage an open examination of the ways organizations are conceived and managed?

- How can OD focus on the drivers of change external to individuals, such as the external environment, business strategy, organization change, and culture change, as well as on the drivers of change internal to individuals, such as individual interpretations of culture, behavior, style, and mindset?

- How much should OD be part of the competencies of all leaders and how much should it be the sole domain of professionally trained, career-oriented OD practitioners?

What Is the Purpose of This Series?

This series is intended to provide current thinking about OD as a field and to provide practical approaches based on sound theory and research. It is targeted for full-time external or internal OD practitioners; top executives in charge of enterprise-wide change; and managers, HR practitioners, training and development professionals, and others who have responsibility for change in organizational and trans-organizational settings. At the same time, these books will be directed toward cutting-edge thinking and state-of-the-art approaches. In some cases, the ideas, approaches, or techniques described are still evolving, so the books are intended to open up dialogue.

We know that the books in this series will provide a leading forum for thought-provoking dialogue within the OD field.

About the Board Members

David Bradford is senior lecturer in organizational behavior at the Graduate School of Business, Stanford University, Palo Alto, California. He is co-author (with Allan R. Cohen) of *Managing for Excellence, Influence Without Authority*, and *POWER UP: Transforming Organizations Through Shared Leadership*.

W. Warner Burke is professor of psychology and education and chair of the Department of Organization and Leadership at Teachers College, Columbia University, New York, New York. His most recent publication is *Business Profiles of Climate Shifts: Profiles of Change Makers* (with William Trahant and Richard Koonce).

Edith Whitfield Seashore is an organization consultant and co-founder (with Morley Segal) of AUNTL Masters Program in Organization Development. She is co-author of *What Did You Say?* and *The Art of Giving and Receiving Feedback* and co-editor of *The Promise of Diversity*.

Robert Tannenbaum is emeritus professor of development of human systems, Graduate School of Management, University of California, Los Angeles; recipient of Lifetime Achievement Award by the National OD Network. He has published numerous books, including *Human Systems Development* (with Newton Margulies and Fred Massarik).

Christopher G. Worley is director, MSOD Program, Pepperdine University, Malibu, California. He is co-author of *Organization Development and Change* (7th ed.), with Tom Cummings, and of *Integrated Strategic Change,* with David Hitchin and Walter Ross.

Shaolin Zhang is senior manager of organization development for Motorola (China) Electronics Ltd. He received his master's degree in American Studies from Beijing Foreign Studies University, Beijing, China, and holds a Ph.D. in sociology from York University, Toronto, Canada.

For my parents,
Annie and Joe Chan

獻 給

媽媽：林 汝 鶯

爸爸：陳 耀 祖

Acknowledgments

I ACKNOWLEDGE MY DEBT to Joseph Campbell for the radiance of his mythic imagination. I sincerely thank people in organizations who included me in their change journeys.

In writing this book, I have benefited from the thoughtful editorial assistance of Derek Allen, Andy Marshall, Kris Quade, Susan Rachmeler, Bill Rothwell, and Roland Sullivan. I appreciate the help of Kathleen Dolan Davies, Josh Blatter, Jeanenne Ray, Dawn Kilgore, and others at Jossey-Bass/Pfeiffer.

I thank Charles Seashore, Holly Benkert, Geoff Bellman, and John Carter for their timely advice.

I appreciate insights from colleagues I've met through the Fielding Institute; the Organization Development Network conferences; the International Society for Intercultural Education, Training and Research; the NTL Institute for Applied Behavioral Sciences; the Alberta Society for Human Resources and Organization Development; the University of Calgary; the University of Regina; and the Journey Circle.

Many people have helped shape my cultural journeys. I thank Nancy Adler, Monica Armour, Steve Bell, George Campbell, Argentine Craig, Patricia Dawson, David Ellerington, Layton Fisher, Jim Frideres, Lanny Fritz, Matt Hamabata, Yoshi Hotta, Margaret Kelsch, Carol Laurich, Robert Marshak, Will McWhinney, Peter Park, George Renwick, Delores Ritchie, T. Don Stacy, Robert Tobin, Jody Veroff, Susie Veroff, Maureen Walsh, and members of my extended families in China, England, and the Americas.

I want to express my love and gratitude to my husband, Derek Allen, for his steadfast guidance and support, and to Avril Ping-Wah and Patrick Cze Wai for their joy and laughter.

Guiding
Change
Journeys

Introduction

THE GLOBAL INFORMATION AGE brings exciting new opportunities to change practitioners—people who facilitate change in organizations. Technological breakthroughs, the spread of new scientific ideas, and greater diversity in the workforce and marketplace are opening new frontiers. As the pace of change increases, so will the demand for people who can guide organizations through frontier territory. However, for practitioners, the new developments also pose a dilemma: How do you guide others when you yourself are unclear about the roads ahead? How do you facilitate transformation in uncharted territory? Where can you find guidance for uncertain change journeys?

Guiding Change

Today's change practitioners are deeply concerned with helping organizations respond effectively to the complex global environment. They are committed to finding change approaches that can address complexity, diversity, and volatility. They want to help build teams and organizations that respect and reflect diversity in cultures, ethnicity, talents, preferences, and life experiences. Their goal is to help guide organizations wisely and creatively.

For change practitioners, the growing diversity in organizations prompts us to reflect on the assumptions of our own practices and consider how best to work with our clients. In this book, I share with you my own attempt to address the issue of diversity and volatility. I learned that it was not just about adopting a new model, whether it be based on ancient wisdom or the latest science. It is about personal change and connections to people. We don't stand outside the process. We go through many of the same struggles as our clients in dealing with change. As a result, we become more sensitive to the impact of our practice on others.

Impasse and Inspiration

This book grew out of my own impasse as a change practitioner. At that time, I was dealing with cancer in my own life and numerous restructurings in my client organizations. As I struggled with my dilemma, I had a sudden inspiration. I realized that all the various *journeys* that I and others experience have common themes. Despite the countless variations of individual journeys, they contain recurrent and enduring characteristics.

The words "archetypal journey" came into my head. What I was thinking of was an Archetypal Change Journey—change patterns that transcend personal and cultural boundaries (Allen, 1995b, 1996a). Further transcendent forces led me to the library, where I discovered and read Joseph Campbell's (1968) work on mythology. These change patterns, I learned, had been around for a long time. The archetypal hero's journey was as old as human history.

In *The Hero with a Thousand Faces,* Campbell (1968) uses the journey metaphor to evoke the complexity and volatility of epochal change. Heroic figures, from Ulysses in European culture to Sheung Ngaw, the Chinese moon goddess, are the personification of the creative life force in every individual and in society. Campbell confirmed what I had intuitively stumbled on already, that each one of us is like a mythological hero or heroine: We have our own particular and memorable journeys to pursue. But when we tell the story of our change experiences, an enduring and consistent framework emerges.

By turning to mythology, new science, and diverse cultural traditions, I was able to move out of impasse and venture into new territories.

Guiding Change Journeys

The purpose of this book is to address the challenge of guiding organization change journeys in turbulent times. It offers you stories, perspectives, practices, methods, and easy-to-use techniques on guiding transformation processes in organizations. I combine insights from mythology, new science, diverse cultural perspectives, organization development (OD), psychology, and different wisdom traditions to create a synergistic approach to organization transformation. Synergistic, here, means *intermeshing disparate ideas and energies to produce something different and original.* My first aim is that you will take the ideas and tools presented in this book and combine them with your own knowledge, situations, and experiences to create new and wonderful innovations. As change becomes more complex, a synergistic approach can help you guide change journeys with greater creativity and confidence.

What You Will Learn

You will learn about an Archetypal Change Journey (ACJ) approach to transformation in organizations. Archetypal means recurring or enduring patterns or motifs. Archetypal Change Journeys are recurring transformation processes and patterns found across many cultures and times (Campbell, 1968).

Specifically, you will learn about eight recurring change cycles and their associated challenges, practices, and methods. The first change cycle is about *inertia* and how you can re-mobilize the creative energy in organizations through awakening practices. In the second cycle, you will learn about answering the *call* to journey and the practice of pathfinding. In the third cycle, you will learn the practice of adventuring to help you and your organization risk a *jump* that will lead to higher levels of awareness and functioning. The fourth cycle will show you how to dance with the dragons of *trials.* Dragons are barriers that obstruct organization change. In the fifth cycle, *dissolution,* you will learn how the practice of compassion can help you shape the turning point in organization transformation. The sixth cycle gives you *discovery.* You will learn about three great epiphanies—revelatory insights that transform low-level goals and energies into higher consciousness and effective functioning. The seventh cycle is about *integration,* combining diversity to create new possibilities and synergies to achieve profitable goals. The eighth cycle invites you to look at *application* and community. You will learn methods to spread your innovations to a broader constituency. By completing the eight cycles, you will achieve the purpose of the Archetypal Change Journey—expanding awareness and competence amidst turbulence and complexity. Figure I.1, The Change Mandala, presents the eight change cycles and practices. A mandala is a roughly circular figure symbolizing a self-organizing universe.

Figure I.1. The Change Mandala

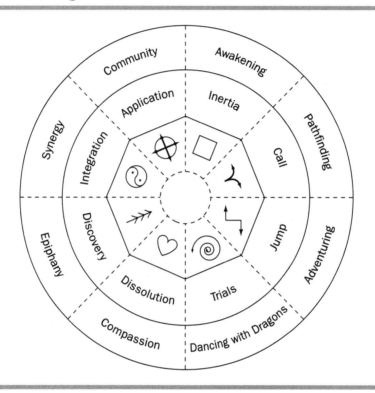

While learning about the change cycles, you will meet change practitioners and organizational leaders who struggle with complexity and diversity. You will travel with organizations that are in the throes of transformation. You will see how they learn to take small steps and to use simple techniques to make a difference in their changing worlds. The organizations and practitioners are composite cases/characters designed to highlight perennial change challenges and situations. The universal themes in their stories will give you insights and strategies to guide personal and organization change journeys.

Mythic Power

The Archetypal Change Journey method is inspired by Joseph Campbell's work on cross-cultural mythology. Having lived in different cultures, I am drawn to Campbell's cross-cultural perspective. I view mythology as a collection of cultural stories about the diverse adventures of the human spirit and its creativity. I adapted the change journey idea from Campbell's *A Hero with a Thousand Faces* (1968). Campbell suggests that the heroic figures in myth are personifications of the creative energies alive in all human systems. Despite changing sciences and varied local cultures that give the heroic figure a thousand different faces, the patterns of transformation are remarkably similar. In my view, Campbell's interpretation of the creative energy is consistent with new scientific insights on self-organizing systems (Wheatley, 1994). Campbell's ideas, especially through *The Power of Myth* (Campbell & Moyers, 1988), the American public television series, have popularized the relevance of the mythic imagination for our times.

My second aim in this book is to apply the power of mythic imagination to organization transformation. I do that by translating some timeless mythic insights into practical perspectives, practices, and methods. I also try to show that both men and women from diverse backgrounds can facilitate "heroic" organization transformation in the here and now. They don't necessarily have to embark on special voyages to far-off lands to effect transformation.

Dialogue on Change

My third aim is to contribute to dialogues on organization diversity (Cross, Katz, Miller, & Seashore, 1994), synergy (Adler, 1980; Arrien, 1998), and the use of self as an instrument of change (Bellman, 1990; Curran, Seashore, & Welp, 1995). I believe my cultural experiences have given me a special point of view. I am interested in sharing what I know about diversity, synergy, and the use of self and in finding out what you know so that we can foster a community of practice (Allee, 2000).

Globalization and the information revolution have transformed our planet into a one-world multicultural community. Today's organizations have to work across multiple cultures to meet the needs of a diversifying workforce, customer base, and community (Adler, 1995; Librizzi & Cadario, 2000; Tobin, 1999). Creating synergy out of diversity can expand common ground and enrich our shared heritage. This book builds on the diversity theme throughout.

Guiding Change Journeys elaborates an important organization development concept—the use of self as an instrument of change. The use of self means that, for change agents, the most powerful way they can influence individuals and organizations is by their own awareness and conduct. This book emphasizes the intertwining transformation journeys of change agents and the organizations in which they work. I invite you to join the dialogues and contribute to synergy.

Who Should Read This Book?

This book is intended for change practitioners—people who create, lead, facilitate, or execute change in organizations. These change practitioners may be managers, change facilitators, team leaders and members, corporate executives, board members, human resource professionals, social advocates, or any kind of change agent. The book can help you guide journeys from multiple cultural perspectives and with anticipation and poise.

How the Book Is Organized

In Chapter One, The Arts of Practicing Change, I discuss three different approaches to practicing change in organizations: classic OD, classic Confucian, and the Archetypal Change Journey (ACJ) approach. The merits of these three approaches are exemplified by practitioners Daryn, Hingram, and Arente in a composite case story. I outline guidelines on using the ACJ approach in your change practice. The last section connects ACJ to change literature.

Chapter Two, Guiding Organization Change Journeys, presents transformation insights in the form of a working Archetypal Change Theory (ACT) and the eight cycles of archetypal change. You will learn to use the technique of Journey Mapping and see its applications to TCom, a composite company, and its CEO, Arthur Jay. You will find the ACJ Survey Questionnaire, tips, and guidelines. This chapter shows you how to use ACJ in practical situations.

Chapter Three, Inertia and Awakening, describes how you can use awakening practices to get out of impasse and re-activate the creative energy in organizations. You look at how TCom uses the techniques of de-centering and re-centering to arise from *inertia* and unleash new creative energies.

Chapter Four, Call and Pathfinding, explains how people and organizations can be called to journey through chance encounters. I highlight the importance of clear change intention in finding an effective change path. I describe and illustrate three pathfinding techniques.

Chapter Five, Jump and Adventuring, tells the story of the intertwining journeys of Julee, TCom's human resources manager, and her companies, TCom and Linco. You learn how Julee embraces the uncertainty of *jump* and takes her organizations to a higher level of awareness and functioning. In this chapter, Julee collaborates with practitioners Daryn, Hingram, and Arente to promote diversity change. They use the Diversity Systems Matrix to survey diversity capacity.

Chapter Six, Trials and Dancing with Dragons, presents the challenges of facing *trials* in transformation. Dancing with dragons will show you how to work with distracting energies or dragons. I introduce the Lotus Path, a method for increasing your understanding of powerful but neglected change energies, such as greed, lethargy, authentic realization, and community. You will learn to apply the Lotus Path through Dragon Quiz, Integrating the Dragons, and Down the Pit.

In Chapter Seven, Dissolution and Compassion, you will focus on the challenges of breaking out of limiting patterns and adopting creative ones. Insights from the Tibetan tradition and new sciences are drawn on to increase your appreciation of *dissolution* and the practice of compassion in organizations. You will discover how compassion can empower change. You will apply the Karmic Change Method (KCM) and the Scripts in Our Heads method to shape the turning points in transformation.

Chapter Eight, Discovery and Epiphany, shows you how to use the seven energy centers of the Lotus Path to transform low-level goals and energies into higher-level awareness and functioning. You learn about the three great epiphanies of radiance, rapture, and bliss and how they can effect fast change. I illustrate the Three Turns of Transformation method through the stories of TradCo, BlissTrek.com, and practitioner Daryn.

Chapter Nine, Integration and Synergy, describes the challenges of intermeshing different ideas and energies to create new wholes. I explore why synergy is integral to creativity and transformation. You learn how practitioner Hingram guides Arthur Jay to use the Seven Synergy Steps to improve relationships with his managers and his organization. The case stories will illustrate the use of Synergy Dialogues and Synergy Symposium in small and large group settings.

Chapter Ten, Application and Community, describes the challenges of facing indifference and skepticism when you try to share new ideas and innovations. You learn six practices that can balance individual freedom with community renewal. The Circles Process method shows you how to include diversity and create community in transitory gatherings. The Sacred Canopy method, adapted from sociological research, shows you how to facilitate meaning and purpose in changing organizations. Sacred Canopy reminds you to connect change with its impact on real people.

Epilogue, the Gifts of Change, looks back at the journey presented in this book and reviews its purpose and aims. You learn that, by completing the eight change cycles, you have expanded consciousness and competence. You will find a handy matrix that summarizes the change cycles and practices. I conclude by reflecting on my own writing journey and inviting you to further the dialogue on synergistic change.

How to Read the Book

This book can be read in two different ways. You can read it in a linear sequence. Or you can pick out the chapter that most appeals to you as a starting point. Chapters One and Two are useful for gaining an overall sense of the book. May you have a productive journey.

Following is a glossary of terms that you will encounter in this book.

Glossary

Archetypal Change A self-organizing process by which a living system fulfills its own creative transformation.

Archetypal Change Journey (ACJ) An approach to human systems transformation that integrates insights from mythology, new science, Taoism, cultural perspectives, psychology, sociology, and organization change literature.

Archetypal Change Systems (ACS) Refers to people and organizations and their abilities to orchestrate the fulfillment of their own creative intentions.

Change Archetype A universal energy pattern or tendency that manifests itself in various forms, qualities, shapes, or processes.

Arrow Archetype A type of change archetype in which energy orients a system in volatility and directs it to achieve goals.

Spiral Archetype A type of change archetype in which energy centers a system in volatility and fulfills purpose through unfolding and enfolding change.

Change Cycles The eight universal patterns of transformation or self-organizing change processes.

Collective Unconscious A term used by Carl Jung (1969) to describe the deep layer of the psyche that is common to all humanity. It is a source of archetypal energy and intelligence.

Enlightenment Illuminating joyful experiences; higher consciousness.

Epiphanies Life-changing insights; flashes of revelation.

Journey Mapping A method of using the eight change cycles to create case-specific change journeys.

Karmic Change A process for altering the effect of cultural programming.

Metaphor A figure of speech that evokes one thing in terms of another.

Quantum Field Webs of intelligence; void of creative potential.

Self-Awareness The ability to know one's own nature.

Self-Organizing A characteristic of the ability of all living systems to self-generate structures that fulfill their own creative purpose.

Synergy Innovative outcome from creative interaction of diversity.

Transcendence Overcoming limiting awareness and functioning.

Transformation A process whereby one state of awareness and functioning becomes another; realization of creative potential.

Worldviews Mental models or paradigms on what is real and how the world operates.

Author's Note

I am aware of criticisms of bias in Joseph Campbell's work. Although Campbell emphasized and highlighted the feminine in his theory of myth, and this before the spread of the feminist perspective, a certain male bias can be found in his mythic interpretations (Downing, 1990). Clyde Ford (1999) points out that Campbell did not adequately explore the rich mythic tradition of Africa. Several scholars have also drawn attention to Campbell's preference for the mystical/universal versus the literal/particular aspect of myth (Noel, 1990). My own reading of Campbell is that, while he did value the universal and the commonality of mythic and spiritual themes, he also emphasized that the universal is only accessible through local and particular manifestations.

1

The Arts of Practicing Change

THE NEEDS OF OUR BURGEONING MULTICULTURAL organizations invite practitioners to consider new change approaches and practices. In this chapter, you will look at three different approaches to practicing change in organizations: classic OD, classic Confucian, and the Archetypal Change Journey (ACJ) approach. You will meet three practitioners—Daryn, Hingram, and Arente—who exemplify these three approaches. You will be introduced to our composite case organization, TCom, and its change challenges. You will learn how Daryn, Hingram, and Arente work with TCom to address the challenges. Before looking at the different approaches, I will first describe the transformation pattern that inspired my Archetypal Change Journey approach—Joseph Campbell's (1968) classic heroic journey. You will look at two common cultural manifestations of the Archetypal Change Journey and how they influence change practices. Last, I show how the ACJ approach links with change literature.

Classic Change Journey

The basic structure of the heroic journey, as described by Campbell, comes in three parts. In the first part, the hero or heroine is at home in a familiar world, but has been called to set out on a journey. Similarly, you may be called to break away from comfortable routines and set out on a metaphorical journey, such as adapting to demands of the new economy or meeting the needs of a vastly different clientele.

Once you take the first step, you are committed to the second—a process of transformation. Just as the hero or heroine stumbles into weird landscapes and encounters fearsome monsters, you soon find yourself in a startlingly different environment with all kinds of perils and pitfalls. If you and your organization are to truly change, there is no avoiding this disturbing yet exhilarating experience. Incomprehensible powers guide the hero or heroine to enter the dragon's lair and risk everything to snatch pearls from the dragon's jaws. Similarly, you are guided to take risks, and by transcending your self-imposed limitations, you are able to grasp treasures of a different kind—knowledge, insights, stratagems, and so on.

You now have to complete the third part of the heroic journey. Bearing your newly acquired treasures, you return to the familiar world and use them to benefit the greater community.

The basic archetypal pattern of transformation has been celebrated in literature, folk tales, and popular culture. Dante's (Taylor & Finley, 1997) *Divine Comedy*, John Bunyan's (1922) *Pilgrim's Progress*, the Chinese folk tale, *The Journey to the West* (Wu, 1984), and George Lucas's *Star Wars* movies are just some examples. Throughout this book, you will see how practitioners and organizations transform this classic journey into new adventures.

Archetype

Because "archetypal" is such a key term in this book, it warrants further explanation. An *archetype* is a basic idea, image, motif, or tendency that can manifest and embed itself in many forms, qualities, processes, and structures. As Carl Jung (1969) taught us, archetypes are part of the collective unconscious; they are humanity's deep reservoir of intelligence. I use the term more specifically to denote an enduring pattern of transformation that will come at you over and over again in your various heroic journeys. In that sense, it represents the creative energy in all of us as we embrace the opportunities and trials of change.

Just as an archetype can manifest itself in many forms and structures, the Archetypal Change Journey can take different shapes, directions, and foci. In the next section, I describe two common cultural manifestations of the Archetypal Change Journey and how they can shape change in organizations.

East Meets West

The globalization process brings people from many different cultural backgrounds together. They carry differing assumptions about why change occurs and how change ought to occur. Born and raised in Asia and having studied and worked in Europe, the United States, and Canada, I am always mindful that I am dealing with people whose assumptions are not the same as my own. We approach and experience change in very different ways.

I now refer to two distinct paths for change that influenced the point of departure for the Archetypal Change Journey, the basis of this book. They are Lewin's classic organization development (OD) model, grounded in Western thinking, and a Confucian/East Asian model. The classic OD model of "unfreeze—movement—refreeze" emphasizes a linear concept of change. In contrast, the classic Taoist/Confucian model, involving the ceaseless interplay of the feminine yin energy and the masculine yang energy, accentuates a cyclical approach.

In the first stage of Lewin's three-step procedure, the objective is to unlock, unfreeze, or somehow thaw an organization from a frozen state. Step 2 is to move the organization from its current state to a consciously defined and desired future state through planned change interventions. Step 3 is to set up processes to refreeze, stabilize, and sustain the desired future state (Marshak, 1993a). The choice of activities in the three steps will be determined by using what practitioners call the action research model, that is, a series of consultations, data gathering, feedback, and joint action planning between the client system and the change agent.

Lewin's three-step procedure was expanded on and elaborated by Lippitt, Watson, and Westley (Burke, 1987) in their phases of planned change model. In essence, OD can be defined as a process and practice of planned change. Lewin's action research model and his three-step procedure have served OD practitioners well. Since its early days in the 1940s, the OD field has grown by leaps and bounds and has expanded into all kinds of organizational areas and technologies of intervention (Schein & Beckhard, 1987).

The classic OD approach to change is, of course, not universal. It embodies a particular set of assumptions about change. These assumptions reflect the Newtonian scientific paradigm or mental model that has had such a strong influence on Western and industrial societies in the last two centuries, that is, predictable and constant laws govern a mechanistic world.

Marshak (1993a) outlines these assumptions as follows: change occurs in a linear fashion, is a progressive movement toward a more desired state, is a destination-oriented or goal-oriented process, creates disequilibrium or chaos, is planned and managed by people who exist independent of the change situations, and is unusual because the normal state is stability.

But these are not the only change assumptions at work in our global world. Marshak (1993c) describes his OD consulting journey to Korea and how he discovered a whole different world of viewing and practicing change. Marshak, a Lewin descendent, makes contact with the descendents of Confucius. In "Lewin Meets Confucius," Marshak (1993a) compares OD and the Confucian/East Asian models of change.

According to the Eastern model, everything in the universe is made up of the constant ebb and flow of yin and yang, the two archetypal creative energies. Harmony is possible when the energies are in dynamic balance. When they are not, imbalance, stagnation, and disorder result. Harmony is the natural way, the way of Tao. Tao is the Chinese word for way, path, method, or truth. It is the creative or quantum void from which change, order, wealth, health, and other states flow. The condition of an organization or an individual reflects the state of relationship between yin and yang energy. When yin and yang are out of balance, relationships between leaders and employees, among co-workers, or between organizations and customers will be out of balance. The result will depress the health of the organization and its profits.

Relationship or "guanxi" is, therefore, a key in the classic Confucian approach to doing business. Jobs, priorities, projects, and products come and go. What is constant is the dynamic relationships among people and between people and their environment. With good relationships, you get things done. Miscommunication and other mistakes can be rectified. It is important, therefore, to invest in relationships by paying attention to the face or dignity of the person you are dealing with. For example, when individuals make a mistake, they worry not only about the mistake, but how it will impact relationships. A Confucian practitioner first reassures the person that the relationship will continue and then hints at how the mistake can be corrected.

Marshak (1993a) identifies the following assumptions of Eastern models of change: Change is a process that unfolds in an orderly, cyclical sequence; it is journey-oriented; it follows the way of the Tao; it is based on restoring and maintaining harmony; and its practitioners strive to act in harmony with Tao.

As you can see, Lewin and Confucius represent quite different approaches to effecting change. The two sets of assumptions outlined above continue to influence many people in diverse organizations around the world.

The Arrow and the Spiral of Change

To further understand the differences, it will help to examine more closely two common archetypal metaphors for both approaches and how they create cultural and personal differences in change. They are the arrow and the spiral (Nichols, 1991). The arrow metaphor accentuates the linear energy. The spiral accentuates the cyclical energy. Following is a description of their common characteristics.

The arrow culture views time and space as linear. The straight-line arrow of time flies toward the horizon never to return. If time is always disappearing in this way, then time is short, and you had better focus on the task at hand in order to quickly achieve your target of good bottom-line results. Arrow culture values straight talk and direct, to-the-point communication. That means telling it like it is, goal setting, and a sequential, compartmentalized approach to problem solving. The arrow metaphor is useful if you want to prioritize multiple demands and focus divergent organizational resources to achieve your targets. Because it is measurable, it gives you a sense of achievement and creates short-term gratification.

However, the arrow points to a key disadvantage. By encouraging organizations to become very busy in meeting short-term targets, it can miss the big picture of change.

In spiral culture, on the other hand, time is cyclical: It goes, it comes back. Night is followed by a new day, the seasons return, and so on. Because time keeps coming back in this way, there are plenty of chances to get things done. Relationships and the process become as important as the task at hand. Communication is tactful, tentative, discreet, intuitive, and mindful of saving face. Preserving relationships over the long term through reciprocal obligation is critical. The spiral approach to change is holistic because it gives you a perspective on how people, relationships, and things are linked together within a living system. When you direct your change attention repeatedly back to the same point, you help unfold, nurture, and enlarge the awareness of the living, self-organizing processes within you. This intuitive and holistic picture helps you appreciate and deal with complexity. The iterative spiral movement envelops, taking in vital intelligence from the environment and thus enhancing an organization's ability to respond to diversity and volatility. But a key disadvantage of the spiral way is the unpredictable length of time it can take an organization to arrive at clarity and focus. Table 1.1. summarizes the archetypal qualities of the arrow and the spiral.

Table 1.1. Arrow and Spiral Qualities

Arrow Qualities	Spiral Qualities
· Orients a system amidst volatility	· Centers a system amidst volatility
· Focuses disparate energies	· Provides a holistic perspective
· Sequences actions	· Balances complexity
· Helps a system to achieve targets	· Fulfills purpose by unfolding and enfolding
· Prioritizes	· Diversifies

Practical Applications

Now I want to show you the practical application of these approaches to an organization and then compare them with the synergistic approach emerging from the Archetypal Change Theory.

Transformation Company, TCom (a composite company, as are all cases used in this book), has a mandate to grow a thriving global business within five years. With a world-class executive team, top-notch employees, and the backing of an enthusiastic board and shareholders, TCom is poised for success and soon lines up several prospective deals. Although performing well, the executive team seems unable to coordinate its talents and realize its true potential. Moreover, individual team members have recurring bouts of inertia, being down in the dumps and stuck there. The organization also lacks cohesion. And, adding to the pressures, it is part of a sector facing increasing demand for greater social responsibility.

TCom's challenge is riding these wild gyrations of change, while sustaining its performance and focus (Allen, 2000). How can TCom be helped? We will now look at how practitioners Daryn and Hingram approach the case. Daryn adopts the classic OD model. Hingram takes the Confucian model.

Using the traditional three-step process, Daryn sets out to shift TCom from its current paralysis. In the first step, through data collection and analysis, Daryn diagnoses TCom's problems as (1) leadership, (2) its inability to work as a team, and (3) communication. In the second step, Daryn and the client carry out a series of interventions, including clarification of expectations, team building, leadership coaching, and strategic planning sessions. She works with TCom managers and employees to set goals and targets, to create roadmaps to guide the implementation of change. In the third step, the practitioner works with the organization to stabilize the change by monitoring how well the new ways are working.

On the other hand, when Hingram takes on the TCom case with the Confucian model, he follows a series of steps based on other assumptions discussed above. First, understanding the importance of relationships, he assesses whether there is a good fit between himself and the potential client. In this case, Hingram is comfortable in undertaking the case because he was asked by a friend who had worked with TCom's chief executive officer. Hingram wants to be helpful to this common friend. Second, Hingram invests time to cultivate his friendship, first with the CEO and his assistant, and then with the rest of the company. Third, Hingram refrains from offering any programs or special interventions. Instead, he focuses on learning about the organization to gain a sense of what the natural balance is within it. He does that by observing the quality of the interrelationships among people, as well as how they feel about themselves. Fourth, Hingram often uses himself as a go-between to improve the quality of various relationships. He helps people with aggressive energy (strong yang) to tone down their tendencies and people with yielding energy (strong yin) to be more assertive. The intention is to bring more balance within the company and create a dynamic harmony in which change can take place. According to the principles of the Confucian model, he makes relationship the substance of his practice.

It is clear, then, that Daryn and Hingram pursue two quite different approaches. Many people in diverse organizations around the world continue to draw on both models and combinations of these models. The phenomenon of "Lewin Meets Confucius" described by Marshak is no longer an exceptional event. It is daily reality. TCom's workforce is multicultural. There, both Lewin and Confucius will meet

Zilohva, Jarmillo, Duong, Little Crow, Hasham, Singh, Smith, Nkwankpa, and many others. The multicultural workforce brings different assumptions and expectations, of which Lewin and Confucius are but two examples. These assumptions affect how people communicate, make decisions, resolve conflict, solve problems, work as teams, strategize, manage crises, and so on. Diversity affects the whole art of practicing change.

Archetypal Change Journey (ACJ)

The reality of this diversity and the chance to draw on different worldviews are significant aspects of the context in which I developed the Archetypal Change Journey. In this section, I expand on the key ideas and assumptions of this model. Drawing on both the Lewinian and Confucian approaches, I articulate a multifaceted way of responding to the diversity outlined above and of helping me deal with diversity and transformation issues in my own journey as a change practitioner. By using the archetypal journey as my foundation, I have created an approach that can address recurring challenges in both personal and organizational transformation.

The increasing diversity in our workplace presents practitioners with an opportunity to clarify their own change assumptions. Such clarification can lead to unexpected discoveries. These lead, in turn, to more change options and hence to better results in the whole change process. Now, we look at how the concepts of archetype and archetypal journey can create a change approach that deals with diverse change assumptions.

Archetypal Change Assumptions

My experience has shown me that change can indeed occur in a linear or spiral fashion, but also in multiple combinations of directions. This means that people in organizations navigate change in different ways. Thus, there are always multiple journeys at work. When interconnected effectively, the diversity of approach can increase an organization's flexibility and responsiveness to changing conditions. Therefore, a key aspect of using the ACJ approach is to help clients discover and link the multiple journeys that are at work in an organization.

Change can occur as a result of awakening consciousness, as well as through activities and actions. This means that organizations and individuals do not always have to rely on being busy to make things happen. Change through shifting consciousness can occur much faster. As we will discuss later, allowing time for thinking, reflection, blissful experiences, and meditation can dramatically increase breakthroughs. Furthermore, change energy can be guided by the intention to change and change models. This means we can shape change consciously. Accordingly, the ACJ approach emphasizes making distinct and deliberate shifts in consciousness and competence.

In organizations, multiple journeys are going on that can influence each other. That means that we can shift an organization's journey by shifting our own journey. It also means the individuals within a group can go on different journeys, and yet the group can arrive at the same destination or achieve common goals. Therefore, another key emphasis in ACJ is leveraging the reciprocal influence of individual and organization transformation.

Archetypal Change Practitioner

Let me return to our composite company, TCom, and show how the ACJ approach might actually be applied. Here are the key steps that Arente, the practitioner, follows.

Step 1. Arente meets with Julee Jangs, the human resources manager, to find out more about the organization's request for help and the condition it is in. Arente learns that TCom is already committed to work with two other consultants, Daryn and Hingram, to carry out interventions and change processes. These would include such things as cross-functional teamwork, building alliances, relationship improvement, leadership development, and so on. Additionally, TCom is also a participant in its parent company's numerous change initiatives in such activities as re-engineering work processes, cultural change, and diversity training. The various initiatives are based on different change approaches already discussed.

Step 2. Using the Archetypal Change Journey guide you will see later in greater detail, Arente immediately maps out the various change journeys happening in TCom. Arente also does some Journey Mapping for himself. That is, he creates a map of key change challenges to clarify how he wants to work with TCom.

Step 3. Arente proposes to focus his efforts on helping his clients within the organization find their own, unique solutions for effectively integrating and synchronizing the diverse initiatives occurring in TCom. These internal clients include teams, divisions, individual managers, and employees, as well as other stakeholders in the company. Because failure to make breakthroughs leads to the missing of performance targets, the efficacy of this process is measurable. By guiding his clients out of their various impasses, Arente can help to make a bottom-line difference in the company's quarterly performance as well as in its longer-term strategic development.

Step 4. To show more specifically how the Archetypal Change Journey works, Arente first conducts a number of coaching sessions with Julee and the chief executive officer, Arthur Jay. The coaching focuses on their journeys as leaders and how their journeys match and intertwine with the company's change journeys. They learn to do Journey Mapping for themselves and the people they work with.

Step 5. Using the Archetypal Change Journey as a guide, Arente, Arthur, and Julee are able to align their own efforts with the change journey of the whole organization. They agree to some short-term and long-term goals.

Step 6. Arente extends similar coaching services to other managers and employee groups.

Step 7. With Arente's help, Arthur and Julee now organize Journey Mapping sessions to chart change journeys with management teams and other employee groupings. At the company's quarterly retreat, the three co-facilitate a large-group session to interweave the various journeys of the whole system into one common journey. The result is a coherent organizational story.

Step 8. During these steps, Arente introduces more detailed explanations of the eight individual change cycles that make up the Archetypal Change Journey. Learning about these cycles gives the clients tools to move out of immobilizing patterns that can range from paralysis to open conflict. Arente explains concepts I will cover later in greater detail, such as the art of dancing with dragons or creating synergy, all of which help the clients move toward their performance targets.

Step 9. Arente refers again to the Archetypal Change Journey map for quick reviews of the various journeys within the company, including his own. That enables all those within TCom to see the shape and qualities of the emerging journeys. It also prompts discussion and feedback among people and groups.

Although TCom's change initiatives themselves are no different than those in any other organization, what makes the difference for a more successful outcome is the use of the Archetypal Change Journey mapping guide. The journey concept resonates with people because most are familiar with its metaphors. It draws meaning and clarity out of organizational and personal confusion. Indeed, the company enjoys many breakthroughs and surpasses its performance expectations. CEO Arthur and some of his managers are promoted to higher positions and responsibilities.

In Chapter Two, you will see two journey maps of TCom. You will learn the specifics of the eight change cycles and the theory underpinning them, plus techniques and guidelines for Journey Mapping.

The Benefits of ACJ

Using the ACJ guide, change practitioners can coach organizations to connect disparate change events to universal patterns and to devise unique strategies to respond to universal situations. It is the ability to sense the unique and the universal that can lead to breakthrough solutions for boosting productivity. ACJ integrates the qualities of arrow and spiral approaches. As a result, you can access more of the collective wisdom of different cultures. You broaden your repertoire to better meet the needs of a burgeoning multicultural human system. ACJ's emphasis on synergy also helps you work better with diversity. Synergy is the innovative outcome of the creative interaction of diversity. ACJ's change cycles and change practices help build intuitive capacity. In today's fast-paced economy, your intuitive abilities will generate a speedier response to change.

We have looked at the ACJ's key concepts and general applications. I now want to show how the ACJ approach connects with the literature on change.

Archetypal Change and Literature

The ACJ approach draws from several converging streams of thought. The following review connects archetypal change to new trends in organization development.

Archetype and Wholeness

Carl Jung views the human system as developmentally driven toward wholeness. In recent years, the principle of wholeness has been incorporated in new change approaches such as Appreciative Inquiry (Watkins & Mohr, 2001), Open Space (Owen, 1997), Large Group Interventions (Bunker & Alban, 1996), and Future Search (Weisbord & Janoff, 1995). I define "wholeness" as the realization of creative potential. The journey to wholeness is a process of integrating unconscious tendencies with conscious purposes or the coupling of the universal and the unique to create a new whole. Archetypes are essentially vehicles that link or couple individual system transformation to collective transformation. By awakening to the presence of archetypes in our organizational lives, we evoke and align the transformative energies within and without (Jung, 1969).

Jung points out that the idea of the archetype exists in fields such as mythology, psychology, and comparative religion. Archetypal forms or motifs can manifest themselves independent of history and culture. Jung stresses holistic integration of Eastern and Western wisdom, science, art, mythology, and mysticism. Those who held firm to the Newtonian-Cartesian scientific tradition received his approach with skepticism. With the rise of new scientific insights, Jung's holistic ideas are found to be consistent with discoveries in the new physics (Capra, 1982; McManus, 1994). Jung had a strong influence on Joseph Campbell, whose work has been instrumental in popularizing the relevance of the mythic imagination for our times. In Campbell's work, the heroic archetype is the personification of the creative energy from the collective unconscious or universal intelligence. The focus of this book is to articulate the practical steps in our dance with this creative energy.

Archetypes and Creativity

From the perspective of new science, archetypes are universal because they are fundamentally energy and information. New scientific insights from quantum physics, biology, and chaos theory offer us different views of reality than Newtonian compartmentalism (Wheatley, 1994). For example, we learn that at the level of the quantum field, there is nothing but information and energy (Chopra, 1994). This same information and energy permeate all things in our world. Information structures and sustains life (Wheatley, 1994). Information self-organizes order and prompts creative adaptation. In short, information is archetypal intelligence. Conscious awareness can shape this intelligence. The purpose of ACJ is to offer insights and steps to make conscious the awareness and then use the awareness to shape the path of this creative intelligence.

Archetypes and Systems Thinking

The use of archetypes helps organizations to tap into invisible structures that shape behavior and productivity. Peter Senge (1990) sees that the recognition and application of systems archetypes is key to developing a learning organization. Systems archetypes are hidden templates that control events invisibly. These archetypes recur in biology, economics, family therapy, psychology, ecology, political science, and management. Recognizing systemic structures can free us of their control. In Senge's system, using systems archetypes requires some special expertise. In ACJ, the archetypes, such as *journey* and *dance,* are those connected with universal experiences. These universal archetypes help us create order and meaning out of volatile and episodic events. They also provide clues on devising unique strategies in response to universal challenges such as inertia and trials.

Harmonizing Archetypal Energies

The concept of archetypal energy relates to the idea of Tao in East Asian culture. Tao is the Chinese word for the way, the logic, the method, or the process of unfolding and enfolding. Unfolding is one becoming manifold. Enfolding is manifold becoming one. Tao is the archetypal energy of creation and dissolution. Tao is a void, the ultimate reality and unity, a field of emptiness from which all material things flow (Lao Zi, 1998). Tao is manifested in the ceaseless dance of archetypal yin (feminine principle) and yang (masculine principle). Yin and yang are archetypal polarities that can manifest themselves in many forms. In organizations, yin and yang can manifest themselves as yielding and aggressive energies, as in the case of TCom. Yin and yang are positive and negative conditions, tending toward extremes of order or chaos. Harmony arises when yin and yang are in dynamic balance. Disorder and impasse result when they are out of balance. As both order and chaos are part of natural transformation processes, we may effortlessly achieve our creative goals by aligning our change intention with our true nature. Lao Zi, the Taoist sage, refers to effortless transformation as Wu Wei, meaning no action or effortless achievement (Allen, 1997). (See Figure 1.1.)

Figure 1.1. Wu Wei—Effortless Achievement

Yin and yang embody the spiral and arrow archetype, respectively. Synergy is produced when arrow energy and spiral energy are in a creative relationship. When they are misaligned, we suffer impasse, stress, and strife. The concept of Tao is consistent with insights from modern physics on the void of the quantum field and its creativity (Bohm, 1980; Capra, 1982; Zukav, 1980). ACJ builds on Taoist insights in developing organization change artistry.

Archetypal Paths of Change

Will McWhinney (1992) views knowledge about paths of change as critical to resolving complex issues of our times. In his book, *Paths of Change: Strategic Choices for Organizations and Society*, McWhinney discusses two archetypal change paths: renewal and renaissance. Renewal helps a system to correct a deviation from its founding principles and values. An example of renewal is when YumCo, a food company, decided to return to its roots and divest itself of its more recently acquired real estate business. Renaissance helps a system to be reborn with new purpose and meaning. The demise of YZ&Z, a transportation conglomerate, and its subsequent reincarnation as a new media company is an example of change through renaissance. McWhinney points out that these two archetypal paths serve as templates for many intentional change strategies, such as organization development, sociotechnical analysis, and open systems planning. The Archetypal Change Journey embodies both renewal and renaissance paths, as both are common recurring change challenges.

Change Through Metaphors

ACJ uses metaphors to tap into the power of imagination in response to change. Metaphors are word pictures that evoke one thing in terms of another. Journey, jumping off, and dancing with dragons are metaphors. These word pictures can open a different world of approaches to creating change. Gareth Morgan (1986) in his book, *Images of Organization*, demonstrates persuasively the power of metaphor in shaping understanding and actions in organization development. He has observed that there is a close link between images and actions. This suggests that we can shape change outcomes by shaping the images or metaphors we use to think about change. Marshak (1993b) points out that the ability to enter into a client's metaphor can help build rapport and partnership. This can mean that we can accomplish change as quickly as we can change our metaphors. In short, the creative use of metaphors can sharpen our vision and enhance our capacity to effect and enjoy change.

In the above, I have reviewed the connection of the Archetypal Change Journey with converging insights from new science, organization change, mythology, different cultural traditions, and psychology. Building on these insights, I formulate a working Archetypal Change Theory (ACT), which will be described in Chapter Two. The commonality of the insights discussed above stresses the dynamic relation of the universal and the unique, or unity and diversity. This review points to a number of competencies, such as shaping change through conscious intention, awareness of the dance of change energies, skillful use of change paths and change metaphors, and embracing polarities, that are useful in facilitating organization change journeys. These competencies—awareness, skills, or practices—are explored in later chapters. The following practice activities can help you apply some of the concepts discussed in this chapter.

Practice Activities

1. What are the key challenges facing your organization?

2. Identify the key assumptions about change in your organization.

3. Identify the key assumptions about change in your own practice.

4. What are the key ideas that have shaped your approach to change?

Summary and Preview

This chapter introduced the key concepts and assumptions of the Archetypal Change Journey approach. I set the scene by detailing and contrasting two classic approaches to change—the organization development/Lewinian and the Confucian/East Asian model—and briefly discussed the arrow and spiral metaphors. This illustrates the range of change assumptions across cultures and helps explain the range of current approaches to change. I discussed why it is helpful to include a diversity of change assumptions and insights in the practice of change in contemporary multicultural organizations and how ACJ can help organization development practitioners to address diversity. I outlined two practical applications of Lewin and Confucius in the case of TCom and introduced another approach that bridges those polarities, embraces world influences, and forms the foundation of the Archetypal Change Journey (ACJ). After touching on ACJ assumptions, I showed how it could be practically applied to TCom and the benefits it would promote. Last, I discussed key ACJ concepts in the context of change literature.

In the next chapter, you will be introduced to ACJ's eight change cycles. You will look at two applications of the ACJ map with our composite, TCom. You will also learn about a working Archetypal Change Theory (ACT) that practitioners can use to guide organization change.

2

Guiding Organization Change Journeys

BEFORE PRESENTING THE METHODS AND TECHNIQUES of the Archetypal Change Journey (ACJ), I will begin by discussing a working Archetypal Change Theory that integrates the insights from the change literature reviewed in Chapter One. This working theory builds a foundation for what follows. You will see how it can be translated into a practical tool, which I call the Archetypal Change Journey Map. Journey Mapping is a technique for identifying and creating change patterns from data collected through questionnaires. Practitioners can use the map to guide all kinds of organization change journeys. I will then define what I have identified as eight change cycles of the ACJ Map and apply them to TCom, our composite company introduced in Chapter One. I also provide guidelines for using the ACJ Questionnaire and incorporating the ACJ approach into your change practice.

A Working Archetypal Change Theory (ACT)

Because of my cultural experiences and personal preference, I have been particularly drawn toward Taoism, cross-cultural mythology, Jungian psychology, and new science to develop my Archetypal Change Theory. What is exciting is how insights from these fields of knowledge can be integrated to create a fuller understanding of how people and organizations change (Allen, 2000).

New science explains the world quite differently from Newtonian science. Rather than seeing the universe governed by predictable laws, new science gives us fresh, unmechanistic metaphors for what the universe is like. We have not even yet developed the language to describe where new science is taking us. But, as I touched on in Chapter One, we learn from the perspective of new science that, at the level of the quantum field, there is nothing but information and energy in the universe. It is this information and energy that give life to us (Wheatley, 1994). The quantum field has also been described as the creative void of universal intelligence (Chopra, 1990). We all emerge from this void. Taoism teaches us that the void is creative potential. It is a universal intelligence that is one and the same as the intelligence within each of us (Wolinsky, 1993). A vital understanding for this theoretical discussion is that the quantum field or void contains a change intelligence that is self-aware and self-organizing. Self-aware means being conscious of its own nature and activities; self-organizing is its ability to fulfill creative intentions. These two characteristics enable creativity to make quantum leaps—discrete jumps to a higher level of awareness and functioning (Chopra, 1990; Wolinsky, 1993). These discrete jumps can be viewed as a process of transformation.

We see the same patterns in all human systems. I describe people and organizations as Archetypal Change Systems (ACS) because they are identifiable entities that can self-orchestrate the fulfillment of their own creative goals. They can organize their own quantum leaps to higher levels of awareness and functioning. Like all living systems, they embody the change intelligence of the quantum field.

This is where the metaphors from mythology are helpful. Transformation by a quantum jump is celebrated in mythology as the Archetypal Change Journey.

Archetypal Change Systems can continuously self-organize into many forms, shapes, and qualities as they co-evolve with emerging conditions. Hence we have diversity in human beings, cultures, and organizations. This diversity is a celebration of quantum creativity. And, because it arises from the same archetypal source, at the root of diversity is unity or universality. In other words, the differences among Archetypal Change Systems are facets of a binding commonality. This means that, when we embrace differences, we are embracing parts of our own creativity. Committing to diversity helps us to sustain Archetypal Change Systems' self-organizing vitality and facilitates quantum leaps.

Variety is also celebrated in the diversity of change theories, methods, and stories found in human organizations. For example, the heroic stories in mythology from around the world are tales of change told by human beings to express their transformation experiences to themselves. What is celebrated in the heroic stories is the adventure of human creativity. In these stories about transformation journeys, we can identify certain common patterns in creative change. And, as Joseph Campbell (1968) taught us, by following these creative patterns, we can be guided to the fulfillment of our creative purpose. As practitioners of change, we can use these creative change patterns to guide organizations in their transformation journeys. Next, you will look at how these creative patterns manifest themselves and how Archetypal Change Systems use them to orchestrate or self-organize their own transformation journeys.

The Eight Cycles of Archetypal Change

Integrating these insights from new science, mythology, and other change literature, I have been able to identify eight key patterns in transformation journeys. I call these patterns change cycles. The eight cycles are *inertia, call, jump, trials, dissolution, discovery, integration,* and *application.* They were presented in Figure I.1. I will define these terms further as I explain how Archetypal Change Systems use these cycles to meet their creative needs.

As participant-creators in the quantum field, Archetypal Change Systems can continuously generate and adapt to change. However, this creative adaptation can be blocked when systems lose touch with or become unaware of changing intelligence and patterns in their inner and outer environments. The blockage creates *inertia*—we become stuck in the same mindless, self-organizing pattern despite changing conditions. We are on autopilot. Happily, due to the self-correcting and self-organizing nature of Archetypal Change Systems, *inertia* is usually temporary. Inner and outer intelligence will send out signals to prompt people or organizations to experiment with new information or new patterns of thinking and acting. This is the *call.* In mythology, *call* signals often come in the guise of accidental encounters with strangers or strange creatures. The invitation to change disturbs the normal routine. This disturbance is referred to as an awakening. It is an initiation into or revelation of some relevant vision or knowledge.

When people and organizations are awakened from their *inertia,* they are presented with choices. They have to decide what direction they want to take. This is the challenge of pathfinding. People and organizations can retreat to old patterns or they can venture forth into new and unknown territory. Choosing the latter leads to the next cycle I call the *jump.*

Once in unknown territory, people and organizations will encounter a diversity of challenges, characterizing the *trials* cycle. The challenges arise from energies trapped in outmoded self-organizing patterns. In mythologies, these trapped energies may don the shape of fierce dragons or terrifying landscapes. To release the trapped energies and achieve their transformational goals, people and organizations have to wrestle with or even dance with these fearful forces.

However, mythological wisdom tells us that the dragons will only relinquish their treasure when Archetypal Change Systems are willing to let go or dissolve old patterns of self-organization. The *dissolution* cycle can create suffering. Giving up familiar habits and ways of thinking can generate fear and anxiety. This suffering can become a turning point in change.

In mythologies, suffering calls forth compassion from supernatural powers and what is lost can be restored tenfold. From a Taoist view, letting go means allowing exhausted energies to return to the void whence new things can arise. This letting-go can also lead to radiance, rapture, and bliss.

From the perspective of quantum creativity, the dissolution of old energies is part of a new emergence or *discovery.* This is the realization of transformation and the reward of treasures. In mythologies, *discovery* is represented by such metaphors as finding the fountain of life, reaching the Promised Land or Paradise. In mythic tales, *discovery* is experienced as enlightenment or epiphanies—sudden leaps or flashes of life-changing insight. From the perspective of new science, it entails a transition into emergent or higher-order intelligence or consciousness. For people and organizations, *discovery* is the achievement of a change vision or a performance target.

Discovery is far from the end of the story. Archetypal Change Systems' self-organizing intelligence will now try to introduce the newly emergent patterns to their existing inner and outer environments to create a synergistic community. This is the *integration* cycle. The resulting synergy will enable individuals and groups to formally launch new patterns and skills—the *application* cycle. When these patterns and skills become ineffective for changing conditions, Archetypal Change Systems will adapt by self-organizing a new change journey and the cycles begin again.

You can see, then, from the above account how the key ideas of the Archetypal Change Theory are used to explain how people and organizations orchestrate or self-organize their own transformations. This explanation suggests that the eight cycles in change are really creative tests that people and organizations, in collaboration with the quantum field, orchestrate for themselves so that they can more completely fulfill their creative potential. I will now show how these cycles can be applied to TCom, our case organization.

We find in TCom the immobilizing pattern of *inertia.* Despite top-notch skills, the organization suffers from recurrent bouts of impasse. Recognizing this condition, TCom decides to seek help.

The demands of the new economy are a *call* to change for many organizations. In the TCom case, practitioners Daryn, Hingram, and Arente are all called to a new journey when they decide to work with the company. In turn, TCom is being called to change by the new ideas and methods brought in by the practitioners. The new ideas are challenging TCom to *jump* into uncharted territory.

Jump is an irrevocable commitment to a new course. Once made, it is too late to change one's mind. TCom is on its way to new adventures. *Jump* becomes a metaphor for a potentially transformative leap into a new or different level of functioning.

The company is then swept into the turbulence of *trials,* in which familiar perceptions give way to unpredictable outcomes. *Trials* are challenging situations imposed from without or within. The emergence of a new competitor or a self-initiated restructuring may trigger a period of trials for organizations. In TCom's case, a key challenge is to establish successful overseas operations. The purpose of the *trials* cycle is to shake loose from ineffective operating patterns.

The *dissolution* cycle can refer to the death and reincarnation of businesses resulting from mergers, acquisitions, or divestitures. It also refers to metaphorical endings, such as the letting go of self-imposed limitations or old business models. For example, a limiting pattern in TCom is its functional hierarchy. This pattern is affecting TCom's ability to make use of its diverse talents. For TCom to benefit from diversity, the organization has to let go of its tight hierarchical pattern. Letting go not only creates confusion and suffering in the company, but it creates space for new discoveries.

Discovery is accepting new patterns and knowledge. It is the climax in the process of change. Clarity replaces confusion. Change is now viewed as possible. For TCom, *discovery* is recognizing that there are other patterns of organization, such as cross-functional teams, self-directed teams, or networks. But adopting these new patterns creates a new challenge of integration.

In practical terms, *integration* is about incorporating new people and ideas to create a new community in the organization. One *integration* challenge facing TCom is developing a new relationship with its sponsoring company. As TCom shifts its hierarchy, it disturbs its hierarchical relationship with its sponsoring company. Another *integration* challenge TCom has to consider is its relationship with its offshore acquisitions.

In the *application* cycle, diverse people at TCom have to become involved to enact the new patterns. The benefits of change need to be shared with a broader group of people. TCom's *application* challenge is to co-evolve an enterprise with its sponsoring company and offshore acquisitions, in which multiple partners can benefit and flourish.

Archetypal Change Journey Mapping

The significance of these eight cycles is that they can be used to draw a map to indicate the various ways we journey to change. I call this practical tool the Archetypal Change Journey (ACJ) Map. The ACJ Map can help people and organizations to discover their own creative intentions and design their own change itineraries. They can custom-plan specific journeys to reach their personal and organizational goals. Now we will look at how to use ACJ maps to orient an organization in turbulence, helping it to stay centered and still able to make proper choices. The eight cycles focus conflicting energies toward concerted action and common goals. Below are three figures showing a classic spiral version, a random flow version, and a classic arrow version of the Journey Map. The purpose of the three representations is to reinforce the notion that change can occur in multiple directions. The arrow, the random flow, and the spiral are three archetypal examples. As you become more familiar with the material in this book, you can discover new territories and draw new maps.

In the Spiral Journey Map (Figure 2.1), I've drawn eight circles to represent the eight change cycles. Each circle represents a distinct state or pattern of consciousness and functioning. You can improve the effectiveness of a particular pattern by directing your attention within each circle. This within-circle approach is similar to Marshak's (1993a) within-pattern change or McWhinney's (1992) renewal path. If you want to change the pattern, you can move from one circle to another circle. Shifting from one circle to another represents a discrete jump in consciousness and functioning. This discrete jump is similar to Marshak's (1993a) cross-pattern change or McWhinney's (1992) renaissance path. The eight circles are arranged in a circular way to evoke the cyclical nature of spiral transformation.

Figure 2.1. Spiral Journey Map

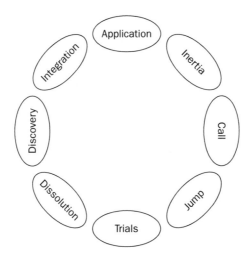

In the Random Flow Journey Map (Figure 2.2), I've drawn circles clustering, overlapping, and free-floating. I want these configurations to convey that the different change cycles can interact with each other in interesting and unpredictable ways to create new journeys.

Figure 2.2. Random Flow Journey Map

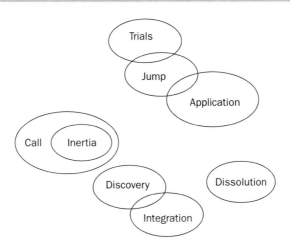

In the Arrow Journey Map (Figure 2.3), I have drawn the graph using a plateau (inertia), a hill (call), a cliff (jump), difficult terrain (trials), a pit (dissolution), a tree (discovery), steps up (integration), and a higher plateau (application) to convey the cycle metaphors. My arrow landscape is just one of many possible pictorial representations. You can choose your own symbols and invent your own graphic landscape.

I generally use the Spiral Journey Map for doing in-depth work in specific change cycles, the Random Flow Journey Map to help me imagine new journey possibilities, and the Arrow Journey Map to design case-specific journeys. As you work with ACJ, you can find new ways of using these journey maps.

A relatively simple process for finding your bearings and direction during upheaval, Journey Mapping can help you pick patterns and meanings out of episodic events. When done interactively with groups, the process can help weave the different change priorities, initiatives, and journeys into a coherent story. The resulting story in turn can guide, co-ordinate, and synchronize disparate actions. To elicit relevant information for Journey Mapping, you can use the ACJ Survey Questionnaire in Exhibit 2.1. The questionnaire is open-ended and can be self-administered or done through group or individual interviews.

Figure 2.3. Arrow Journey Map

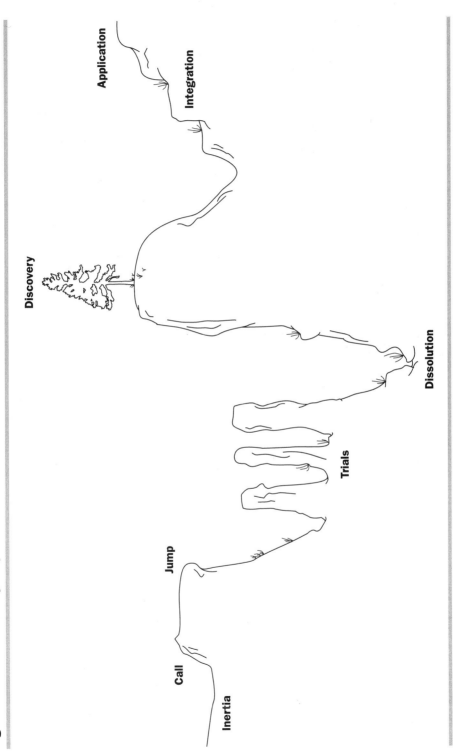

Adapted in part from *The Hero with a Thousand Faces* by Joseph Campbell (1968). Princeton, NJ: Princeton University Press.

Exhibit 2.1. ACJ Survey Questionnaire

Instructions: (1) Identify the system being addressed; this can be the whole organization, a division, a network, a team, or an individual. (2) Respond to each question. Make your answers vivid by including facts, feelings, wishes, and your imagination.

The system under focus is _____

Awakening from Inertia: Overcoming Impasse

• What patterns are immobilizing the creative energy in your system?

• What is keeping these patterns going?

• What specific impact do these patterns have on your system?

Call to Journey: Invitation to a New Course of Transformation

• What is motivating the creative energy in the system now?

• Who or what is doing the calling?

• What new directions does your system want to explore?

Jumping into the Unknown: Irrevocable Commitment to a New Course of Change

• What new energy is lurking in the unknown?

Exhibit 2.1. ACJ Survey Questionnaire, Cont'd

- What or where is the unknown for your system?

- What constitutes a quantum leap for your system?

Facing Trials and Dragons: Confronting Negative and Positive Change Energies

- What are the change dragons in your system?

- What are the patterns that trap creative energies?

- What strategies do you have for unleashing trapped energies?

Dissolution: Letting Go of Self-Limiting Patterns

- What patterns of thought, feelings, attitude, and action must be let go?

- What new patterns do you want to generate?

- What systems can you put in place to support letting go?

Discovery: Accepting New Patterns, Knowledge, and Experiences

- What are the conditions that promote bliss and laughter in your system right now?

Exhibit 2.1. ACJ Survey Questionnaire, Cont'd

· What new realities or visions does your system want to create?

· What life-giving experiences do people in your system want to have more of?

Integration: Creating Synergy Out of Diverse Energies and Patterns

· What are the newly emergent patterns or energies?

· What strategies will be used to integrate these new patterns or energies?

· How will you create synergy out of diversity?

Application: Enacting New Patterns to Spread Synergy and Creativity

· How will the new patterns be enacted?

· What strategies will be used to involve others and spread the innovations?

· How will the benefits of change be shared with the larger community?

Practical Applications

Now that we have looked at the tools and techniques of the Archetypal Change Journey, we can see their practical application to TCom, our composite case. Let's now pick up TCom's story from the perspective of Arthur Jay, the CEO.

▶ Application: From Functional Expert to Executive Leader

Thirty-six months ago, Arthur Jay, an international explorer, interviewed for an executive position with TCom. He accepted the challenge of taking TCom international and moved his family from the United States to Canada. Six months into his new job, he felt stuck and unable to persuade his organization to take major initiatives. He was caught between recruiting a new, world-class team or keeping the staff he inherited. He feared being derided as a "ruthless American" or dismissed as a "gutless wimp." He felt time was ticking by and that he was not delivering expected results.

Arthur Jay's Leadership Journey

Using the ACJ Survey Questionnaire and Journey Mapping steps and techniques, Arente and Arthur created the following journey. A map of this journey is shown in Figure 2.4.

Inertia—What Is Immobilizing the Creative Energy?

- Cultural shock.
- Fear of being labeled.

Call—What Is Motivating the Creative Energy?

- Grow a new type of international organization.

Jump—What New Energy Is Lurking in the Unknown?

- Creating a new world-class team.
- Prospecting for deals.
- Being a leader of a whole organization.

Trials—What Are the Dragons That
Must Be Faced to Unleash the New Energy?

- Feeling fears of rejection and appearing incompetent.

- Juggling multiple tasks of prospecting, team building, growing an organization.

- Struggling with polarities: jumping in and holding back.

Dissolution—What Old Energies
Must Be Let Go Before the New Can Emerge?

- Dealing with remorse related to firing of employees.

- Giving up limiting stereotypes.

- Reaching beyond functional expertise.

Discovery—What New Patterns
Must Be Accepted for the New System to Grow?

- Success in attracting several world-class managers and employees.

- Leadership as new territory for exploration and blissful experience.

- The joy of being part of a like-minded yet diverse team.

Integration—What Adjustments
Must Be Made to Sustain the Discovery?

- Embrace the multiple realities of leadership.

- Create synergy within himself and in his organization.

Application—How Will the New Gifts
Be Used to Renew the Community?

- Use presidency to implement an inclusive and empowering global energy company.

Figure 2.4. From Functional Expert to Executive Leader

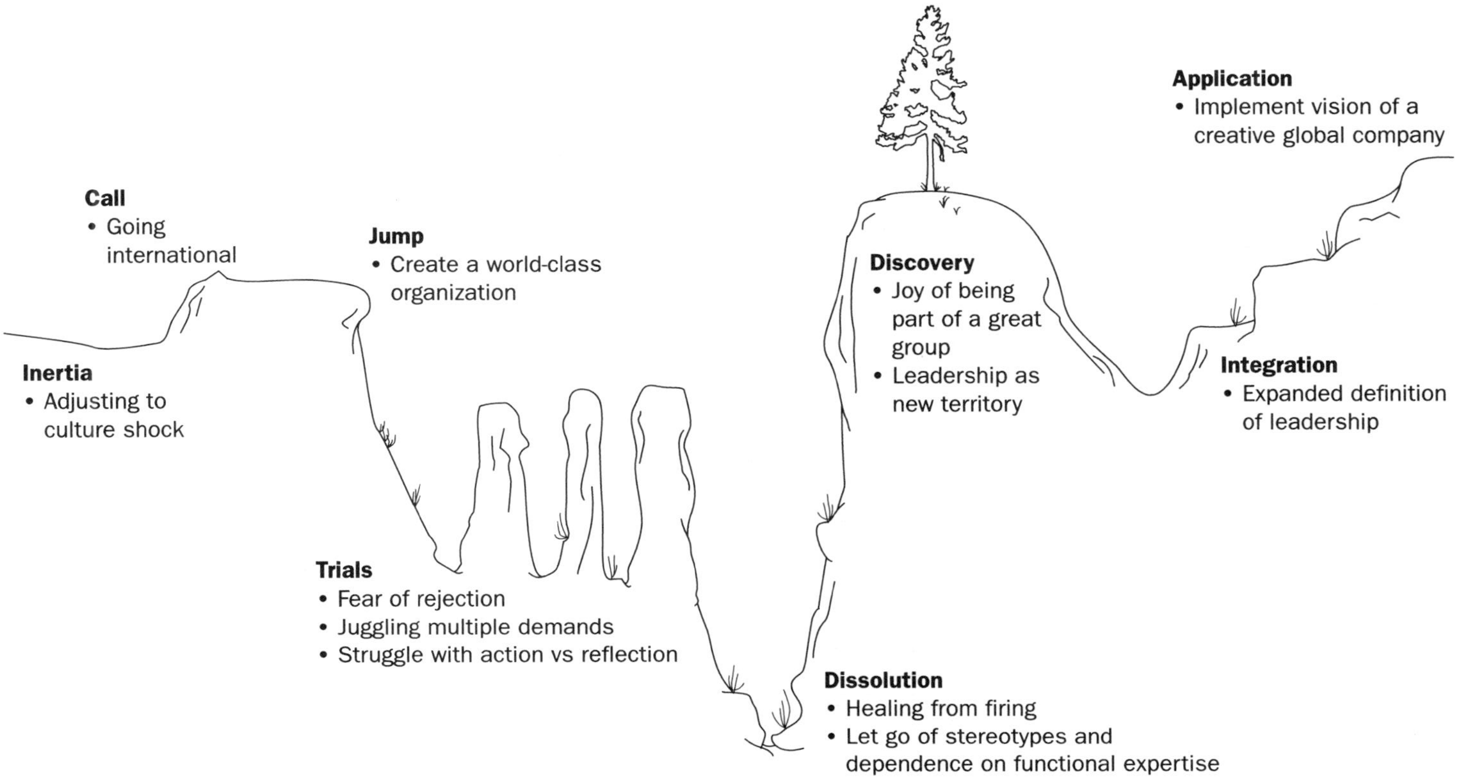

Call
• Going international

Inertia
• Adjusting to culture shock

Jump
• Create a world-class organization

Trials
• Fear of rejection
• Juggling multiple demands
• Struggle with action vs reflection

Discovery
• Joy of being part of a great group
• Leadership as new territory

Dissolution
• Healing from firing
• Let go of stereotypes and dependence on functional expertise

Application
• Implement vision of a creative global company

Integration
• Expanded definition of leadership

Adapted in part from *The Hero with a Thousand Faces* by Joseph Campbell (1968). Princeton, NJ: Princeton University Press.

After working through the ACJ Map, Arthur Jay was able to put his dilemma into perspective. ACJ helped him reframe his experience. Instead of being immobilized by self-doubt and remorse, he began to embrace the impasse as a sign of maturing leadership. The impasse signified the complexity of juggling multiple realities and demands. His journey map helped him to anticipate the trials and discoveries that lay ahead. It showed him that, by participating fully in the unfolding cycles, he was expanding his leadership capacity. By working on his own inertia through small actions and improvisations, Arthur Jay was able to help unleash more of the potential in his managers and in the organization. ◀

Arente also used the Journey Mapping technique with individual managers to chart their own developmental paths. A common question regarding Journey Mapping is whether a system can avoid the pit of *dissolution.* The ACJ Map helps you realize that the pit is a critical part of transformation, so you can embrace it rather than try to avoid it. Following are steps used by Arthur and his managers in their Journey Mapping. You can adapt the same steps in your own Journey Mapping.

Steps in Creating a Journey Map
- Identify the system under focus, for example, individual, team, organization.
- Collect relevant data using the ACJ Survey Questionnaire.
- Organize mapping session; involve interested participants.
- Use the ACJ Map as a guide or template to structure relevant data.
- Use the questions associated with the eight cycles to prompt imagination.
- Clarify change intention. While focusing your attention on the clarified change intention, improvise and tinker with the data until a coherent story emerges. The story represents a new self-organizing pattern.
- Create a new journey map and use it to orient and focus the creative energies in the system under focus.

► Application: From Functional Hierarchy to Network

In the sixteenth month of Arthur Jay's tenure, TCom celebrated a multi-billion-dollar offshore takeover that effectively doubled TCom's size. Internal and external discord over power and control erupted just as the organization was exhausted from months of nonstop pushing. TCom was in a quandary. To help it reorient itself and focus disparate energies, Arente and the executive team met to create a prospective journey for the whole company. Using the eight cycles, the group retraced the developmental path that brought TCom to its current quandary and then identified tasks on the path leading to a desired future.

TCom's Organizational Journey

Following is the journey that the TCom executive and Arente created. A map of this journey is shown in Figure 2.5.

Inertia—What Is Immobilizing the Creative Energy?

- Brilliant explorer assumes leadership.
- Nothing seems to be happening after initial recruitment excitement.
- Explorer-leader stalled.
- Sponsoring company sits back and waits for return on investment.

Call—What Is Motivating the Creative Energy?

- Cultural conflict—pendulum between ruthlessness and indecisiveness.
- Problem with forming a world-class team.

Jump—What New Energy Is Lurking in the Unknown?

- Discovery of new resources.
- Opportunity for big exploration plays, edging out major competitors.
- Firings and recruitment completed, world-class team ready to go.

Trials—What Dragons Must Be Faced?

- From prospecting to operating, TCom must successfully establish operations in overseas locales and show a quick return on investment.

This is an early test of sheer survival. TCom must convert new discoveries into cash flow. In mythological terms, this is a test to find out whether there is real fire in the belly to create something new. If TCom fails to deliver early returns, capital will flee. Is TCom up to it?

- Keep sponsors/investors interested. Can TCom mediate the thrill of prospecting with the thrill of money making? Can TCom create synergy out of diversity? In this test, the system must confront its fear of rejection.

- Creating a sustainable and nimble global business unit. Can TCom compete successfully against well-financed transnational companies? This is a test of efficacious use of creative power. It is a David and Goliath situation. Does TCom have enough confidence and finesse to outsmart the giants?

Dissolution—What Patterns Must Be Let Go?

- Hierarchical mindsets and practices.
- Sorrows and wounds from unsatisfactory conflict resolution.
- Exclusive camaraderie of a small core group.

Discovery—What New Patterns and Gifts Must Be Accepted?

- The power of shared leadership. TCom develops a system that utilizes a diversity of energies: exploring, systems building, profit making, and competent use of power. Such systems cannot evolve if individuals draw only from disciplinary expertise and ego power.

- A "dancing" organization. All TCom employees are key to the success of the business. Depending on the project and situational demands, select employees form a core, with others in supporting roles. The movement from core to support is open, fluid, and responsive.

- A common ground of shared mystical experience. Employees and investors see themselves as partners in discovery and creation. Both derive thrills from risk, going by their "gut feelings," discovering and creating something new.

Integration—What Adjustments
Must Be Made to Sustain the New Patterns?

- TCom works out its relationship with its sponsoring company. This requires patience and skills. The international company assumes increasing importance for the original company. A common move is to replace the business unit founder with an administrator. Knowing this through Prospective Journey Mapping, TCom will have to take into account the problem of leadership in its stabilizing phase.

- Stabilizing operations. TCom balances between flux and stability to support responsiveness and continuity.

- Work/home balance. Employees establish healthy routines and balance to minimize start-up burnout.

Application—How Will the Gifts Be
Used to Create a Synergistic Community?

- TCom enacts its visions and values to create a responsive global network.

- TCom shows leadership in embracing profit and social responsibility.

- TCom applies creativity to invent a new company for the global information age.

TCom had worked primarily as a collection of individuals and entities. In the absence of a shared organization story, the familiar functional hierarchy dominated by default. The ACJ Map provided a guiding template to weave individual dreams, needs, and contributions into a whole system story. The ACJ Map served as a common framework for identifying organizational tasks that must be undertaken to transform TCom from a promising start-up to a confident operator. The ACJ Map did not provide direct answers, but it forced the organization to confront the issues of survival, affiliation, and power with realism and imagination. Journey Mapping helped TCom realize that it is not enough to win in the acquisition of quality assets, employees, or business entities. The company also needed to grow an organizational vision and form to convert diversity into synergy and assets into cash flow.

Figure 2.5. From Functional Hierarchy to Network

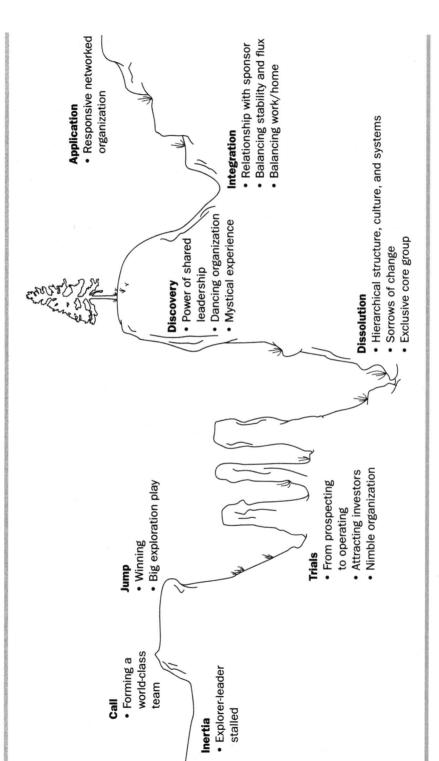

Call
• Forming a world-class team

Inertia
• Explorer-leader stalled

Jump
• Winning
• Big exploration play

Trials
• From prospecting to operating
• Attracting investors
• Nimble organization

Discovery
• Power of shared leadership
• Dancing organization
• Mystical experience

Dissolution
• Hierarchical structure, culture, and systems
• Sorrows of change
• Exclusive core group

Application
• Responsive networked organization

Integration
• Relationship with sponsor
• Balancing stability and flux
• Balancing work/home

Adapted in part from *The Hero with a Thousand Faces* by Joseph Campbell (1968). Princeton, NJ: Princeton University Press.

Journey Mapping helped TCom to bring to the surface the unspoken desire to create a great inclusive group and to promote excellence, synergy, and community. The ACJ Map provided a focus for ongoing conversation and improvisation. Participation in mapping gave managers and employees a chance to contribute to the central plot lines as well as act out numerous supporting stories. They realized that individual and organizational journeys are mutually influencing and can be mutually enhancing.

To help people in TCom use the Journey Mapping techniques effectively, Arente shared the following tips. ◀

Journey Mapping Tips

- Journey Mapping can be used to interpret the past, present, and future. For prospective maps, use the future tense. For retrospective maps, use the past or perfect tenses. You can map past, present, and future developments by using different tenses in one map.

- The Archetypal Change Journey is cyclical. You can use any cycle as your starting point for analysis and intervention.

- When collecting data for mapping, apply appreciative awareness to the system under focus. Appreciative awareness means studying a system with a positive and open attitude, gently embracing both what is life-giving and what is not. In short, keep an open mind and let the data surface.

- Clarify your change intention and hold the intention while mapping. Improvise and tinker until choices and meaning emerge.

- Journey Mapping can be done individually or in small or large groups.

- Journey Mapping is storytelling; use your creative intent to shape the plot line and outcome.

In the foregoing, I applied the Journey Mapping technique to two levels of change in TCom: individual and organizational. The two applications illustrate that change journeys at different levels are mutually influencing. Journey Mapping shows that behind turbulence and impasse lie logic and self-organization. By tracing episodic events and situations onto the ACJ Map, individuals, teams, and organizations can improvise and tinker with their desired destiny. They can stay focused and retain different options, even as they negotiate the steep peaks and valleys of change.

Archetypal Change Journey Guidelines

ACJ is most useful as an integrative framework to coordinate and keep track of multiple change initiatives or journeys in organizations. For example, in TCom's case, ACJ was used to create a coherent organization change journey out of the diverse initiatives from individual and group journeys. This means that no matter what change approaches an organization uses—Appreciative Inquiry, Open Space, Complexity Science, Re-engineering—ACJ can support the process and help individuals and organizations to coordinate their disparate journeys. ACJ offers a second-order perspective to the multiple changes occurring in organizations. Such a perspective allows the organization to see the change work in progress. Because ACJ is evolved from enduring change patterns, using it as an anchor helps people to connect seemingly episodic and confusing events to universal human experiences. ACJ can be used with individuals, teams, or large groups. In later chapters, you will learn more about different ways to use ACJ.

ACJ is also useful in coaching individuals and teams. The eight change cycles provide a meaningful structure that moves people from impasse to breakthroughs. As ACJ is a self-organizing process for achieving creative intentions, individuals and teams can use it to discover retrospective journeys and design prospective journeys to reach their change goals.

A good way to incorporate ACJ into your practice is by trying its theory, methods, and techniques first for yourself. Then, as an observer, you can practice Journey Mapping on other systems—your organization, teams you're involved with, your family, and so on. You can also journey map stories in books, films, and TV shows. When you are confident about using it, apply it to your client situations. Following is a list of user guidelines.

- Get acquainted with ACJ theory, methods, tools, and techniques;

- Study the tools and techniques included in examples of practical applications;

- Practice applying the approaches, tools, and techniques to your own situations and observations;

- Adapt the approaches, tools, and techniques to meet your own and your clients' needs. ACJ uses concepts from new science and mythology. You may need to translate ACJ terminology to match your clients' language use; and

- Use ACJ as a framework for guiding and monitoring your own change agent journey.

Following the above guidelines can help you start using ACJ right away. To further your ability to use ACJ, you can incorporate additional ACJ concepts and tools discussed in later chapters into your change practice.

In the foregoing, you have looked at the theory, concepts, techniques, and applications of the ACJ approach. In the remaining chapters, we will look more closely at each of the eight change cycles. You will learn more about the change challenges associated with each cycle and the practices you can use to meet the challenges. You'll get hands-on practice with some interesting methods, tools, and techniques drawn from different cultural traditions. You will look at case examples that show you how you can apply ACJ cycles in your organizations. You will also learn more about the change journeys of TCom and its people.

Last, to refresh your learning from this chapter, you may want to do the following practice activities.

Practice Activities

1. Select a system you are interested in and fill out the ACJ Questionnaire in Exhibit 2.1 for that system.

2. Using the data collected in your ACJ Questionnaire, create a journey map for the system you selected.

Summary and Preview

In this chapter, I presented a working Archetypal Change Theory (ACT) to frame the approach I take to organization development. You learned about a practical tool derived from ACT called ACJ Mapping. I defined and described ACJ's eight change cycles and how they can be practically applied. I provided guidelines and tips on using the ACJ Survey Questionnaire to elicit information and for Journey Mapping—a process for creating case-specific change journeys for individuals, teams, or organizations. You looked at two applications of Journey Mapping with TCom. The two cases show the intertwining influence of individual and organization change. I discussed how practitioners can adapt the ACJ approach in their practice. To learn more about how to use each of ACJ's eight change cycles, I now invite you to embark on your first change cycle—Awakening from Inertia. You will learn how insights from our working Archetypal Change Theory can cast new light on impasse and change.

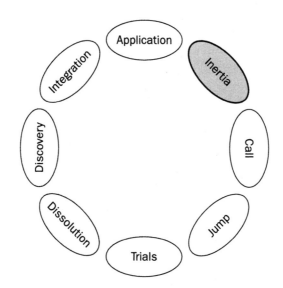

What pattern is immobilizing the creative energy?

Inertia and Awakening

THE DRAMATIC TRANSFORMATION of our business and communications systems through globalization leaves many organizations and individuals frozen at the edge of change. This state of impasse characterizes the Inertia Cycle, which forms the first of the eight cycles of the Archetypal Change Journey (ACJ). For change agents working with stalled organizations, the challenge is to help them shift out of inertia and discover new possibilities. Organizations and individuals can discover and orchestrate their own breakthroughs to navigate the currents of change that are sweeping the world. They can progress to different ways of thinking and acting despite the overwhelming situations they may find themselves in. Because people and organizations are Archetypal Change Systems (ACS), they all have the ability to adapt to the turbulence around them.

Because mythology from all cultures has common roots in the universal, creative intelligence, I refer again in this chapter to mythological examples. I will use mythology to cast new light on inertia and describe practices that can facilitate shifts out of the impasse. You will look at how TCom experiences inertia and how this composite company orchestrates its own quantum leaps into new ways of operating. Readers will be given a simple method, "de-centering and re-centering" that organizations can use to shift out of limiting patterns. Because the Inertia Cycle and the Call Cycle are closely connected, both are mentioned in some instances in this chapter. In Chapter Four, you will look at the Call Cycle in greater detail.

Inertia Cycle

In the creative evolution of people and organizations, the Inertia Cycle is the experience of being stuck in one mode of self-organization. In classical physics, inertia refers to the tendency of matter to remain at rest if at rest or, if moving, to keep moving in the same direction, unless affected by some outside force. From the perspective of new science, inertia can be viewed as a near equilibrium state or a state of maximum entropy or decay (Prigogine & Stengers, 1984).

In the Archetypal Change Journey, inertia is a natural prelude to quantum leaps. Inertia implies that an organization or individual—an Archetypal Change System (ACS)—is asleep or mindlessly repeating an outmoded pattern of thinking and acting. Using a fairy tale analogy, the kingdom is overgrown with entangling weeds and thorny thickets. No one can come or go. The exchange of energy or information is blocked. The potential of the kingdom remains undeveloped. The talents of the citizens are wasted. The whole place lies dormant, waiting for an inner stirring or outside intervention. Inertia is invariably the starting point of a change story. The "once-upon-a-time" opening in fairy tales signals that things have been quiet but are about to change. Inertia can be viewed as an incubating period for creativity and rebirth.

The Awakening

According to the Archetypal Change Theory, when an ACS is stuck in this way, it sends out messages that it wants to do things differently. This is the *call* for help. The signals include impasse, quandary, lethargy, stress, internal conflict, looking for quick fixes, outbursts, hostility, and overt violence. They are the preludes to the awakening or the awareness of different realities and possibilities. To awake is to arouse, stir, or move the senses from a state of sleep to a state of wakefulness. The response to the call occurs either as an internal awakening or as an external guide. Forces within the ACS or from the outside will provide the inspiration for considering new paths.

In mythologies, awakening is a form of initiation. The eyes are opened to hidden mystery, seeing options and alternatives where none existed before. The veil of ignorance is lifted. Curiosity and hope rekindle the creative fire within. The system is ready to shift out of automatic pilot. The story of Prince Arjuna and Lord Krishna from the Hindu tradition provides an example of the relationship between inertia and the awakening guide. Beset by civil war, Prince Arjuna feels immobilized and unable to go into battle. He is trapped by the dilemma of seeing family and friends in both armies. The opposing armies are a metaphor for polarities, a classic mythological motif in transformation tales. Steering a way between apparently irreconcilable opposing forces is the archetypal challenge for all mythological heroes and heroines (Campbell,1993).

The call for help to find a way out sets the stage for Lord Krishna (in the guise of Arjuna's charioteer) to begin the divine teaching that is the *Bagavad Gita.* The awakening guide advises that, as a leader, Arjuna's job is to mobilize his creative energy, move out of paralysis, and do battle, however dire the consequences. The injunction is to venture forth, even if the going is tough and unpredictable. What Lord Krishna does is to provide a different perspective from which to see the world.

The lesson of this story is that, as intelligent systems, organizations and people know how to orchestrate help to remove themselves from impasse. This help is usually right within or around them. However, the help or feedback you receive is not always the kind you want to hear. For example, Lord Krishna does not tell Prince Arjuna he is excused from going forth to battle or that the outcome will be predictable and safe. Confronting fears and jumping into the unknown are part of transformation. The prince, fearing his call to action might cause himself or others to be killed, is an archetypal metaphor for the chief executive officer or the change agent in an organization. Conventional wisdom suggests it is not appropriate for them to admit fear and ask, "Can I really move forward?" However, acknowledging the dilemma triggers others to come forward with new ways. While the chief executive officer and the change agent have the creative energy for change within them, they are not omniscient alone. If they think they can predict the outcome, they are playing God and cutting themselves off from the universal creative intelligence. In TCom's case, Julee, Daryn, Hingram, and Arente are acting as awakening guides. They have picked up on TCom's call and respond with new ideas and perspectives.

Awakening Practices

Let's look at some practices that can facilitate awakening for stalled organizations.

First, watch out for call signals. Change practitioners and those interested in transforming their organizations can facilitate awakening by paying attention to the symptoms we discussed earlier in this chapter.

Second, it is useful to reconnect with past creativity within the organization or the individual. However stuck an ACS may be now, it has a history of creative adaptation. Using the Journey Map introduced in Chapter Two, you can help an ACS to retrace its past creative paths to breakthroughs. That will boost confidence that it can do so again.

Discovering self-organizing patterns is a third practice for helping the awakening process. As I have explained, inertia is induced when an ACS mindlessly repeats patterns that are not congruent with current conditions. You can help to shift the ACS from inertia by pointing out the patterns you have observed and inviting the client to explore the effectiveness of these patterns. Through awakening, movement in a new direction is possible and desirable. I will provide more information on how to use this technique later in this chapter.

Fourth, you can then show the ACS other worlds or ways of conducting itself. An ACS is stuck when it becomes disconnected from change conditions within and without. This disconnect shields the system from seeing other worlds that exist. (By worlds I mean the particular ways individuals, groups, or organizations perceive and experience current realities and the methods they use to respond to the realities.) By giving information on different worlds within and outside of the organization, you can stir imagination and raise curiosity. Benchmarking or measuring the system's performance on best practices is one way to show other worlds. Another way is to provide information on new change paradigms, such as Appreciative Inquiry (Watkins & Mohr, 2001), complexity science (Olson & Eoyang, 2001), or other models discussed in this series.

A fifth and significant practice to prompt awakening is what I call "de-centering and re-centering" (Allen, 1999). I will first give a general description of what this entails. Later in the chapter, under the technique heading, I will provide a more detailed step-by-step guide to its practical application. *De-centering* means to remove a rigid pattern from the core or center of an ACS. The pattern may be a self-organizing process involving ideas, individuals, or a group. You can initiate de-centering by asking the client or group to draw a circle to represent their organizational world. Then, ask them to put in the circle a guiding principle, value, person, situation, or goal that dominates that particular world. De-centering means removing the dominating pattern from the circle. The client then engages in *re-centering* by drawing a new circle and placing a new, creative, and inspiring guiding idea or goal inside it. Experiment with applying this idea to the organization and see what happens. For example, as you will see, a rigid pattern in a work team can be the acceptance of the team leader or manager as the sole source of creativity among the participants. De-centering and re-centering would result in team members removing the boss as the only input and replacing him or her with the team's vision and ideas.

The technique of de-centering and re-centering illustrates that sometimes only small changes are needed to disturb a system's habitual and limiting self-organizing pattern. By taking small actions, change agents can help a system become aware of its own gaps of perception and break the pattern that sustains inertia.

When people and organizations are stuck, it is important to realize that they may feel embarrassed and fearful of being judged. You can help lessen the distress by applying the sixth practice, which I call "appreciative awareness." This practice means witnessing a system's impasse with mindfulness, openness, and loving kindness, characteristics we don't always associate with a corporate setting. It entails participants' being nonjudgmental and filling their hearts with a gentle and reflective acceptance. These kinds of feelings are helpful because they then alert the system to new self-organizing possibilities.

When we pay appreciative attention to a human system, we call forth the life energy in that system. Our witnessing gaze brings a world into being. In Hindu mythology, Vishnu, the dreamer of the universe, opens his eyes, and a whole new world comes to be (Campbell, 1990). As change agents, we all have the power of awakening vision. Through our attentive gaze, the seventh practice, we activate the change intelligence and shape it. To discover our own creative, self-organizing logic, we have only to cast our reflective gaze on our own doings. Our internal logic will then reveal itself. Once the logic is revealed, we have a choice. Do we want to continue with the old logic or do we replace it with logic more consistent with our new vision? When we enact a new logic, we bring forth a renewed world.

Inertia happens when an ACS stops improvising. To awaken such a system, change agents can encourage it to re-engage with improvisation and tinkering, the eighth practice. This can be achieved by infusing new information into the system to disturb its habituated self-organizing patterns and invite it to tinker with new ways.

The ACJ Map and Questionnaire

Before concluding the eight practices for awakening, let me remind the reader that a key purpose of the Archetypal Change Journey Map is to awaken the creative energy in organizations and people. When they are stuck, they can be shown how to use the ACJ Map and ACJ Questionnaire outlined in Chapter Two. By seeing their current quandary framed as part of a change journey, people can make sense of the dilemmas before them and feel hopeful about progress and change. Questions such as "What pattern of thinking, feeling, or action is immobilizing you?" can sometimes stop people from repeating an immobilizing pattern.

Techniques for Awakening

As suggested earlier, small actions, a bit of new information, or even just one question can awaken a system from inertia. In this section, I will describe two easy-to-use techniques for awakening. The first is de-centering and re-centering and the second one is Worlds at Work.

De-Centering and Re-Centering

Earlier, I described de-centering and re-centering as an awakening practice. Let's look at the actual steps for using this practice.

1. Identify the system/situation under focus.

2. Draw a circle to represent the system.

3. Identify the dominating or rigid pattern that guides the creative energy in the system. This pattern can be a principle, idea, value, feeling, behavior, or person. Write this pattern in the center of the circle. The resulting graphic is a symbol for the current self-organizing pattern.

4. The participants talk about the impact of this dominating pattern and their experiences with this pattern. Participants identify how this pattern contributes to their quandary.

5. Draw another circle representing the system without the current dominating pattern in it.

6. Participants brainstorm what new pattern may be productive for the system. Write or draw this pattern in the center of the new circle.

7. Participants talk about how this pattern will help them become more creative and what experiences they expect to have in this new system.

Exhibit 3.1. is a handy worksheet to help you apply this awakening technique.

Exhibit 3.1. De-Centering/Re-Centering Worksheet

Step 1. Identify the system/situation under focus.

Step 2. Draw a circle to represent the system.

Step 3. Identify the immobilizing pattern. Write or draw this pattern in the center of the circle.

Step 4. Identify the specific ways the identified dominating pattern contributes to a quandary.

Step 5. Draw another circle representing the system without the current dominating pattern in it.

Step 6. Brainstorm a new guiding pattern. Write or draw this pattern in the center of the new circle.

Step 7. Envision the positive impact of the new pattern.

Let's now look at the awakening experiences of our case organization, TCom, and how it uses awakening techniques to shift out of inertia.

► Application: TCom's Awakening

From the Archetypal Change Journey perspective, the hiring of Arthur Jay (AJ) was a shift out of inertia for the organization. Prior to AJ's arrival, TCom was a stalled organization—an international company only in name. In substance, the old leadership was hesitant about sending employees overseas or establishing any significant offshore presence. Once in place, AJ heralded a new era. Quite quickly, TCom established itself as an international organization. TCom's international success was, in essence, a quantum leap, possible because its new leaders had a different vision and a clear intention to go international. However, the realization of TCom's goal created new dynamics in its internal and external environments. For example, TCom's sudden growth put tremendous demands on its internal business systems and relationships. The company had to self-organize solutions, such as more hiring or developing integrative systems and procedures to match the emergent conditions. The functional hierarchies within TCom and its sponsoring company were also under stress. Boundaries, roles, responsibilities, communication, decision making, lines of authority, and conflict management were all called into question. Externally, TCom's offshore success put the company on the energy industry's radar screen, affecting its own and its competitors' strategic moves. TCom became a player to be watched.

These internal and external developments created new conditions for self-organization within TCom and in relation to its sponsoring company, its competitors, and the communities in which it operated. The goal of internationalization alone became too limiting for the emerging conditions. Once again, TCom fell into a quandary. The company struggled for ways to organize itself to fit with its changing intentions and environments.

A big issue for the company was AJ's frequent absences. His managers felt immobilized in their decision making whenever he was out of town. In effect, AJ and his organization were acting out or co-creating what I describe as a solar pattern. AJ was the sun in the center, around which everyone revolved. He was the giver of life, and without him people felt dull and in limbo. People relied on him for guidance, approval, affection, and a sense of worth.

Why did people put AJ in the center? Because they believed he, as CEO, should be there. AJ also kept himself there by holding on to decision-making and approval functions. Instead of working as a unit, group members relied on a series of bilateral relationships. The group was frequently trapped in impasse. To help the group members discover their own way out of inertia, Arente and Julee showed them how to apply the de-centering/re-centering steps to their solar system:

Step 1. Identify the system under focus: TCom's relational system.

Step 2. Draw a circle.

Step 3. Identify the immobilizing pattern: The dominating pattern is AJ as the sun in the middle, with bilateral relationships with his managers.

Step 4. Identify the ways this pattern contributes to the quandary: Managers feel immobilized in AJ's absence. They are unsure about their colleagues.

Step 5. Draw a new circle.

Step 6. Brainstorm a new guiding pattern: The group feels no one person should dominate the center. Instead, the guiding center should be the group's vision and strategic priorities. The new image is that of a circle of leaders, including AJ, all facing the guiding center.

Step 7. Envision the positive impact: The group expects to feel re-energized and to be able to work toward shared visions and priorities.

The group found that, whenever they were stuck, they could use the de-centering/re-centering technique to move out of impasse. ◀

Next, we'll look at the second awakening technique.

Worlds at Work

This is a simple observation technique. At a meeting, observe the interaction among the participants. Draw a graphic to represent how they connect within the room. Mark how many times each person talks and, using arrows, whom he or she talks to. For example, when A talks to B, draw an arrow going from A to B. If A talks to the center of the room, draw an arrow going from A to the center. By the end of the meeting, you should have a detailed graphic on the pattern(s) of inter-action and exchange. These patterns show how the group is self-organizing its own creativity. Show the pattern(s) to the group and have a conversation about its implications for their quandary. Explore with the group members what other patterns they can self-organize.

Here we introduce another case company named ICO. This company is working hard to foster an innovative culture. At an ICO staff meeting, I observe that the flow of communication is more web-like when the boss is out of the room. That is, everyone participates and everyone interacts with each other. The graphic is a dense mass of crisscrossing arrows. However, the pattern becomes a hierarchical funnel when the boss is in the room. The exchange occurs one way between the boss and individual workers. The graphic shows the boss as the key originator of arrows to the different employees. Employees respond to the boss, but seldom initiate communication with one another. After seeing the graphs, the group members decide to explore why they have two different patterns.

I've found that observing Worlds at Work can quickly help clients to awaken to the patterns they co-create. The Worlds at Work technique can be used when coaching a group or an individual. You can show the client how to use the technique or use the technique and show the resulting observed patterns to the client. The following are three common self-organizing patterns I've observed and shown to ICO and other organizations.

- *Solitudes:* Some employees are not linked into the core process or group, so they find themselves not having enough work or the right kind of work. Some are in limbo because there are issues about their performance and future.

- *Funnel:* In project or proposal meetings, participants contribute views and opinions along specialized channels to a manager. There is little interaction among channels. The manager acts as facilitator and collector. Yet, everyone in the room is capable of doing what the manager does.

- *Web:* When a deadline is coming up, employees from different units scramble to complete the work. The focus is on communicating with all parts of the system to get needed data and resources online and offline. In organizations with good cross-functional communication and in networked organizations, employees interact freely with one another, creating dense webs.

Figure 3.1. shows the three different worlds at work.

Figure 3.1. Worlds at Work

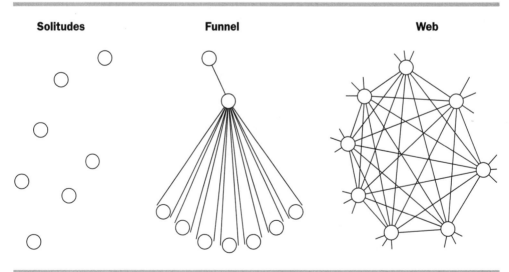

We have looked at two easy-to-use awakening techniques. You may now want to have some hands-on experience with them by trying the practice activities.

Practice Activities

1. Observe and record the energy patterns in your system. Show them to the group. Ask participants to talk about the patterns. If coaching individuals, ask them why they participate in those patterns. Ask them whether the patterns are helpful and, if not, how they can be changed.

2. Apply the seven steps of de-centering and re-centering to your organization. After you identify the current dominant pattern, ask yourself how this pattern affects your work as a change agent. How have you contributed to the current pattern? After you re-center the organization with a new liberating pattern, ask yourself how this new pattern will affect your work as a change agent. How can you contribute to this new pattern?

3. Apply the seven steps to your personal development. What is the dominant pattern guiding you? What is the guiding pattern that you would like in your circle?

Summary and Preview

In this chapter, I applied the Archetypal Change Theory and mythological insights to understand inertia and how organizations experience impasse. A key insight is the ability of people and organizations to self-organize breakthroughs from inertia. A question or a new piece of information can disturb an immobilizing routine. I described eight practices that can facilitate awakening in organizations, and we looked at how TCom experienced and moved from its quandary. Two easy-to-use awakening techniques and illustrations were provided.

Once a system has awakened from inertia, it is ready to embark on a new course. In the next chapter, you will learn more about the Call Cycle and techniques for finding change paths.

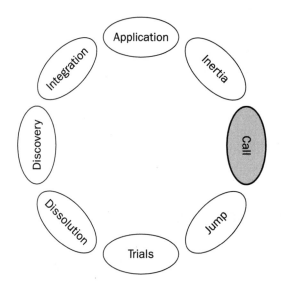

What is motivating the creative energy now?

4

Call and Pathfinding

ON THE LAST CHAPTER, you looked at people and organizations awakening from Inertia. Now you will learn more about the Call Cycle. *Call* is the invitation to a new course of transformation. Once you have answered the call, you have to figure out your change path. That means clarifying your change intention and choosing a change direction. In this book, the tool for pathfinding is the Archetypal Change Journey (ACJ) Map, and the method for pathfinding is Journey Mapping. You have already learned about the ACJ Map and some Journey Mapping applications. In this chapter are more details on how to facilitate a Journey Mapping session. You will look at three Journey Mapping techniques: retrospective, prospective, and continuum.

The Call to Journey

Call is an invitation to commit to a new course of self-organization. According to the Archetypal Change Theory, people and organizations are called to change when they have outgrown their knowledge base and are in need of new learning and development. Call is a signal that there is more creative potential in a system than is being used. The call signals can come from within the system or from the environment. Answering the call to journey sets you on a new path of change. In the transformation of a system, the Call Cycle is a time when the awakened archetypal change energies within and without are on full alert, enticing, pushing, or hinting that a new direction is now available. These unleashed energies can create many reactions, from confusion to exaggerated hopes and fears. A key role for the change agent is to help the organization or system experiencing the call make sense of what's happening and provide directional guidance and support.

In tales of adventure, the start of a new course of change often results from a seemingly accidental encounter with a person, a supernatural being, a strange creature, or some magical objects. For example, Alice's adventures in Wonderland begin when she encounters a pink-eyed white rabbit. In the children's story about the princess and the frog, the princess is strolling in her garden, absent-mindedly playing with a ball. The ball rolls down into the lake, and a frog brings it back to her. This accidental meeting is the prelude to transformation. Take the fable of Jack and the Beanstalk: Jack brings home some worthless beans. His mother tosses out the beans and one of them grows into a mighty beanstalk. The beanstalk, symbol for a path to a higher level of awareness and functioning, leads Jack to discover new strengths and riches. The chance encounters in fables suggest that people and organizations can be called to journey on any day at any time. By availing ourselves of the opportunities, we can fulfill creative goals.

Sometimes, the call to journey can entail a total change in direction. For example, Peter, one of the disciples of Jesus, is called from being a fisherman to become a fisher of people. Gautama Buddha's discovery of the path to enlightenment starts as a casual stroll outside his palace grounds. His unexpected encounters with old age, sickness, and death lead to a new course of transformation for himself and his devotees. Similarly, the spiritual life of Rumi, the Sufi mystic and poet, was transformed in an accidental meeting with a wandering dervish.

In organizations, this accidental encounter can take the form of a dissatisfied customer, the recruitment of a new team member, or the arrival of new competitors on the scene to disturb the routine. The call to journey can come in the guise of new opportunities. A new market is opened up. Enabling legislation is passed or a debilitating regulation is removed that changes the operating environment. As a result, new horizons open up. Brand new markets unfold from a successful product innovation. A new alliance may be in the works. These events alter existing interaction inside and outside the organization and push current perspectives in different directions. The system is invited to pause, look, and listen to what is happening.

It is common in the Call Cycle for an organization to be beset by mistakes and mishaps. Processes that used to work well suddenly stop being effective. Tried-and-true methods do not produce the expected results. People behave in puzzling ways. There is then a tendency to go for quick fixes and stop-gap measures in an attempt to eliminate these annoyances. But mistakes and mishaps are messages from the inner and outer intelligence that the old patterns are inappropriate for emerging conditions. To grow and realize the system's potential, a new way of organizing is needed. How will the system respond?

The response to the call to journey is not automatic. The call is usually not clear-cut. It may be so subtle that it escapes the system's radar screen. Existing patterns of perception and interaction can screen a system from hearing the call to journey. Totally absorbed in its old world, the organization may be oblivious to the emerging conditions. But, when ignored, the call can grow louder, more insistent.

Sometimes, the system hears the call but denies that the call has meaning or implications for its effective organization. A call can be so threatening that it over-powers the system's ability to respond. In this case, you may eliminate the source of this call or get out of the call's way. You kill the messenger because you do not like the message. Sooner or later, though, the call becomes irresistible and you must answer it. Your challenge then becomes finding a path to new ways of living.

Pathfinding Practices

Pathfinding has been an integral feature in the development of human systems. Pathfinding is about choosing a particular course or option out of a range of possibilities to direct your creative energy. As Archetypal Change Systems, we have evolved simple and intricate directional techniques and tools to provide guidance and pinpoint specific courses of action. Clocks, calendars, seasonal festivals, and milestones are examples of directional tools. Our world cultures have also evolved simple and complex systems for pathfinding. Babylonian astrology, I Ching, the Chinese Book of Changes, the Enneagram, the medicine wheel of Aboriginal cultures, the mandala principle of Tantric Buddhism, and the Pollen Path of the Navaho are some examples of pathfinding systems. In our area of interest, the field of organization development (OD) can be regarded as a special directional technology. Its diverse theories and methods are directional schemes and techniques.

The Archetypal Change Journey is such a pathfinding scheme. There are four principal actions in the practice of archetypal pathfinding: create a map, find an orienting device, clarify change intention, and choose an effective route.

Create a Map

A change journey map can help a system survey the change terrain and identify possible paths and destinations. The objective is to help an awakened system deal with multiple stimuli from without and impulses from within. For example, in this book the ACJ Maps depict possible landscapes at the frontiers of change. A change map offers an overview of issues, problems, goals, and means for change. In the book, *The Change Leader's Roadmap,* authors Linda Ackerman Anderson and Dean Anderson (2001) use a model called drivers of change to delineate the scope and extent of forces acting on organization change. Such a model can help an organization realize that the old path, or traditional ways of doing things, will not help it reach new goals. In recent years, the advent of new science is revising the maps of our universe and how the world works. Used with awareness and sensitivity, the new maps can guide us to new territories. As change agents, we want to pay conscious attention to the maps we use to guide change.

Find an Orienting Device

The objective here is to make use of appropriate change technologies to pinpoint new directions with conscious intention. Just as a compass, viewfinder, or radar screen can focus our perceptual field, in organization change, we use metaphorical orienting devices such as change models and concepts to guide intention and energy. For example, in this book, the Archetypal Change Journey is a guiding template or directional aid for finding change paths. Other books in this series use different directional models such as Appreciative Inquiry (Watkins & Mohr, 2001) and complexity science (Olson & Eoyang, 2001). Most directional aids aim at helping a system to activate its own inner guidance system to assess new needs and intentions. As change agents, you can work with organizations to tune into their own inner guidance system. Journey Mapping can serve as a catalyst for sharpening the internal guide.

Clarify Change Intention

A system is called to journey because new needs have arisen in response to emerging conditions. This necessitates a review of the purpose and intention of the organization. A key job in guiding change is to help a system clarify its change intention.

Change intention arises from the creative impulse in a system. This impulse is alive and responsive to changes within and without. You can help a system to articulate the impulse in the form of goals and purpose by asking, "What motivates the creative energy right now?"

Change intention shapes the course and quality of a change journey. Intention is like the needle of a compass. It points you in the right direction no matter what the circumstances. However, fears and conflicting desires can cloud change intention. When a system loses touch with its change intention, it can become stuck and its change effort derailed. In the Trials Cycle, you will learn more about fears and desires that detract from change intention.

Choose an Effective Route

There are many ways to move from one state of being to another. Depending on the needs and means of a system, some routes are better than others. Choosing wisely means creating a continuum that connects the past, present, and future. This continuum serves as a bridge and a route. You can use the ACJ Map as a template to create a suitable continuum and make sense of disruptive developments.

Facilitating Journey Mapping

When a group is ready to embark on a new course of change, a Journey Mapping session provides the focus and opportunity for creative interaction among diverse members. Effective in groups of ten people to a hundred or more, it aims to stimulate the emergence of new organization patterns. Sessions can range from a couple of hours to one day, depending on the purpose. For example, mapping enterprise-wide strategic directions with a diverse group of people who do not work together regularly will take longer. With a team that has frequent contact, the process will be quicker. The following are key steps that you can adapt to meet your purpose:

1. Gather the group. Explain the purpose of the session.

2. Do some warm-up activity appropriate to the group to gather the divergent energies and focus attention. The Opening Circle Activity described in Chapter Ten can be adapted to create a learning community. This is an important step because a key objective of Journey Mapping is to focus conflicting energies toward common change goals.

3. Orient the group to a journey frame of reference by asking all participants to brainstorm the organization/group's key achievements and setbacks in

the last period (six months, one year, ten years, or any duration appropriate to the session's purpose). This exercise should take little time. I usually allow five to ten minutes.

4. Present the ACJ Maps, both the classic spiral and arrow versions. You can also present the random flow version to show how the change cycles can interact with each other. Provide a narrative description of the Archetypal Change Journey, using material on the working Archetypal Change Theory (ACT) and the eight change cycles discussed in Chapter Two. It is not necessary to be comprehensive or explain every concept to its fullest extent. After presenting the concepts, invite the group members to use their own experiences and imagination to expand interpretations of the cycles. Then ask the group members to briefly discuss their insights and reactions, together or in smaller clusters. The discussion will help people to digest the information. Explain that it is not necessary to grasp all the concepts fully, for participants will later have hands-on experience with the material.

5. Explain that the task for the group is to create a change map. Discuss and decide on the system under focus. This could be the organization, a division, a unit, or a product. Show and/or hand out "Steps in Creating a Journey Map" and "Journey Mapping Tips." You will find this material in Chapter Two.

6. Divide into small groups if appropriate. Hand out copies of the ACJ Maps (Figures 2.1, 2.2, and 2.3) and ACJ Questionnaire (Exhibit 2.1) to each participant. Provide the following instructions: "You will now use the ACJ Maps as a guide and create a change map. The system you will focus on is our [organization, division, group, or unit]. Here is the ACJ Questionnaire. By brainstorming answers to the questions in the ACJ Questionnaire, you will tap into your change intention, knowledge, experiences, and imagination. Once you have collected the data (answers), try to see patterns and meanings in them. Using your change intention as a guide, tinker and improvise until meaning and coherence emerge. Create a story out of your meanings and patterns. Draw a graphic picture of the change journey. The resulting graphic can be a classic arrow map, a classic spiral map, a random flow map, or some other variation appropriate to the patterns and meanings you have identified."

7. Ask the small groups to present their journey maps.

8. Following the same procedures and working together, the whole group will now create an overall map.

9. Conduct a group conversation about how each member can participate and support the group's journey. Invite participants to create individual maps to show how they can synchronize with the group journey.

Variation: You can start with the whole group deciding on the focus and the change goal/target.

Tip: You can hand out transparencies for the groups to draw their journey maps and then show them on the overhead projector. By placing the transparencies from all the groups one on top of another, you effectively show the diverse shapes of change journeys. Use Exhibit 4.1 as a Journey Mapping session planner.

Exhibit 4.1. Journey Mapping Session Planner

- Group/Audience:

- Session Purpose:

- Session Outcomes:

- Learning Community Building Activity:

- Orienting Activity: Brainstorm Key Achievements of the Last _____ Months

- Present ACJ Maps: _____ Spiral Map   _____ Arrow Map   _____ Random Flow Map

- Key Themes of ACJ Map Presentation:

- Process for Dividing into Small Groups:

Exhibit 4.1. Journey Mapping Session Planner, Cont'd

· Instructions for Creating Change Maps:

· Handouts: _____ ACJ Maps _____ ACJ Questionnaire _____ Other Material

· Questions for Debriefing Small-Group Presentations of Change Maps:

· Instructions for Creating Whole Group Map:

Exhibit 4.1. Journey Mapping Session Planner, Cont'd

• Instructions for Dialogue on Creating Individual Journey Maps to Support Group Journey:

• Closing Activity:

In Journey Mapping, you can use a different time focus: retrospective (past), prospective (future), or continuum (past, present, and future).

Retrospective Journey Mapping

Retrospective Journey Mapping is useful when you want to reflect back on how a system reached its current situation. By reflecting back, a system can discover its own creative strategies for overcoming impasse, finding a new course, making quantum leaps, and so on. Confusion about going forward can often be clarified by looking back and referencing the past. The purpose here is not to duplicate past success but to help a group to reconnect with its creative energy.

In Retrospective Journey Mapping, you are looking at journeys that have been completed. The retrospective view helps a system learn from its past and enlarge its future. Use the past tense in asking the questions in the ACJ Questionnaire and when following the steps in Journey Mapping and tips on the Journey Map. Figure 4.1 is a sample Retrospective Journey Map.

Figure 4.1. Sample Retrospective Journey Map

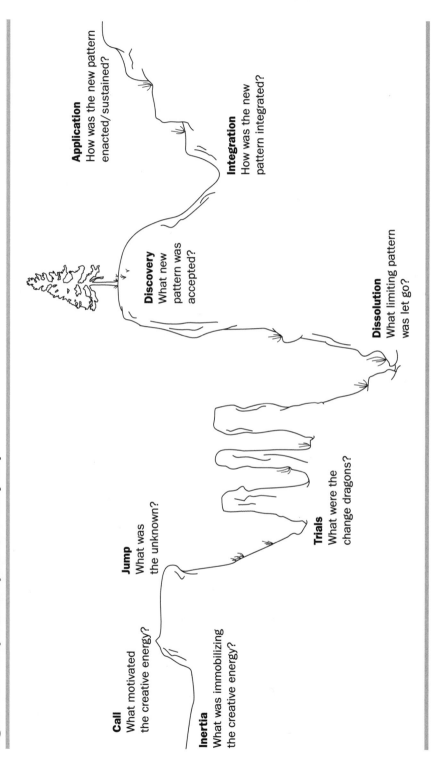

Call
What motivated
the creative energy?

Inertia
What was immobilizing
the creative energy?

Jump
What was
the unknown?

Trials
What were the
change dragons?

Discovery
What new
pattern was
accepted?

Dissolution
What limiting pattern
was let go?

Application
How was the new pattern
enacted/sustained?

Integration
How was the new
pattern integrated?

Adapted in part from *The Hero with a Thousand Faces* by Joseph Campbell (1968). Princeton, NJ: Princeton University Press.

Prospective Journey Mapping

Prospective Journey Mapping is about journeys into the future. It is about creating a desired future in the here and now. Use the technique when you want to clarify and shape a system's future challenges and discoveries. Use the future tense in asking questions in the ACJ Questionnaire. Prospective Journey Mapping can be done individually or as a group. Once a prospective map is created, identify the strategies and concrete steps that need to be taken now to realize the future. Figure 4.2 is a sample Prospective Journey Map.

Continuum Mapping

Use Continuum Mapping when you want to have a sense of continuity in your pathfinding. Use multiple tenses in asking questions in the ACJ Questionnaire. First, decide which of the eight change cycles on the ACJ Map reflects your current situation. To the left of the present cycle is the past; to the right is the future. For example, you may decide your system is in the Trials Cycle. You can then use the present tense in asking questions about trials, for example: "What are the dragons that must be faced now?" and so on. In this case, the past are the jump, the call, and the inertia cycles or some other combination of cycles that capture the experience. Use the past tense to ask questions related to these cycles. For example, what was creating impasse? How was it overcome? The cycles in the future will be dissolution, discovery, integration, and application, or some other combination of cycles that you anticipate. Use the future tense in asking questions related to these cycles, such as, "What new patterns will have to be accepted?" "How will the new and old be integrated?" and so on. Figure 4.3 is a sample Continuum Journey Map, using trials as the current phase. Adjust the tenses accordingly if you select another cycle as the current phase.

The three mapping techniques described above can be used to identify new directions and find change paths. We will now look at TCom's pathfinding experience and applications of the three mapping techniques to a work unit in TCom.

Figure 4.2. Sample Prospective Journey Map

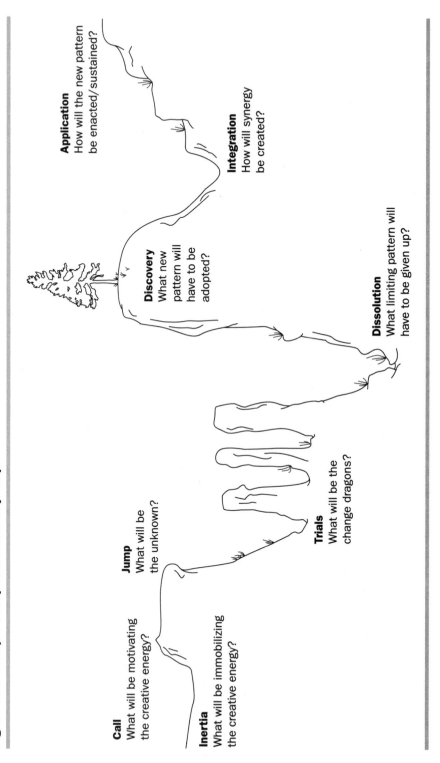

Call
What will be motivating
the creative energy?

Inertia
What will be immobilizing
the creative energy?

Jump
What will be
the unknown?

Trials
What will be the
change dragons?

Dissolution
What limiting pattern will
have to be given up?

Discovery
What new
pattern will
have to be
adopted?

Integration
How will synergy
be created?

Application
How will the new pattern
be enacted/sustained?

Adapted in part from *The Hero with a Thousand Faces* by Joseph Campbell (1968). Princeton, NJ: Princeton University Press.

Figure 4.3. Sample Continuum Journey Map

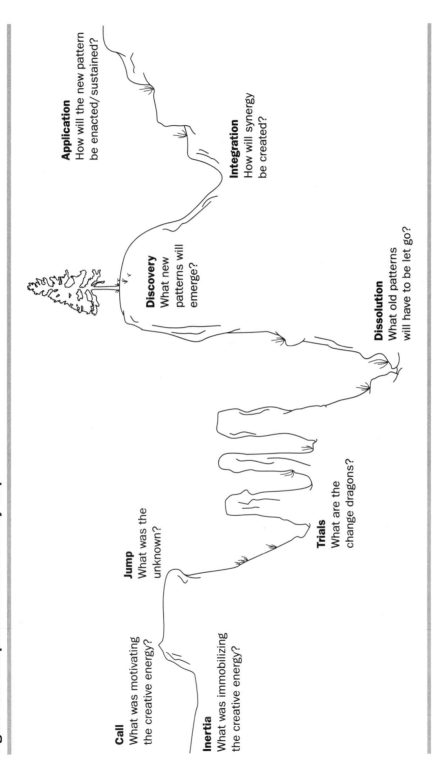

Call
What was motivating the creative energy?

Inertia
What was immobilizing the creative energy?

Jump
What was the unknown?

Trials
What are the change dragons?

Dissolution
What old patterns will have to be let go?

Discovery
What new patterns will emerge?

Integration
How will synergy be created?

Application
How will the new pattern be enacted/sustained?

Adapted in part from *The Hero with a Thousand Faces* by Joseph Campbell (1968). Princeton, NJ: Princeton University Press.

Pathfinding in TCom

What is TCom's experience with call and pathfinding? You may recall that, to overcome impasse, TCom called on the services of practitioners Daryn, Hingram, and
Arente. The practitioners' new perspectives and ideas set TCom on a new course
of transformation. As a result of the encounter, TCom became more choiceful about
finding new ways to adapt to changing conditions.

Journey Mapping provided a quick method for shaping and reshaping possible
change paths. Through Retrospective Journey Mapping, people at TCom have
learned that, although often stuck in a quandary as to what to do next, they can
find ways to move out of successive impasses. Through Prospective Journey Mapping, they know they can intentionally shape their change journey to achieve targets and goals. The Journey Mapping method can be used to assess how new
developments may change the shape of an organization's change journey. They
learn that the path of change cannot be fixed once and for all, but is in a constant
state of evolution. To keep the path from stultifying their creative impulses, they
need to be continually aware of what is going on inside and outside the organization. They realize that sometimes they have to take directions quite contrary to
established routes.

As a result of Journey Mapping work, TCom employees feel less concerned
about coming up with "the one best structure" or "the one best path" because they
now understand that an appropriate structure or path will emerge if they become
clear about their own change intention. Through Journey Mapping, TCom discovers that one of the issues motivating its creative energy is the need to find ways of
smoothing relations between the established and the new parts of the organization.
Now we'll look at how a TCom unit copes with this situation.

▶ Application:
Retrospective Journey Map

In the past year, TCom's Corporate Support Services (CSS) grew by over
500 percent. At first, the staff expansion was a welcome relief for the work
overload. But tension, stress, and conflict soon became apparent. Julee
and Arente facilitated a Journey Mapping session with the unit. The unit
created three journey maps to help search for direction and strategies.
Here's a sample of TCom CSS's Retrospective Journey Map that looks
back at its journey from five years ago to the current situation.

Inertia—What Was Immobilizing the Creative Energy?

- CSS was created five years ago to provide support for TCom's international expansion. Throughout that time, the unit was busy but accomplished little, as TCom was not successful with its international effort.

Call—What Motivated the Creative Energy?

- Arthur Jay arrived on the scene and demanded more innovative services.

Jump—What Was the Unknown?

- CSS went international almost overnight. Staff welcomed the new challenges but felt caught off guard. They responded by working extra hours and sacrificing their personal time such as holidays.

Trials—What Were the Change Dragons?

- CSS struggled with the international work. The members confronted their fears of inadequacy and inexperience and then admitted they needed extra help.

Dissolution—What Limiting Pattern Was Let Go?

- After a lot of struggle, the founding staff of CSS gave up on the idea that they could do it all alone.

Discovery—What New Pattern Was Accepted?

- Their hard work and dedication were rewarded. Their request for new staff was met with approval.

Integration—How Was the New Pattern Integrated?

- To integrate the new employees, the founding staff provided close supervision. They tried to educate the new staff on the rules and norms, just as they had done with other TCom managers and employees.

Application—How Was the New Pattern Enacted or Sustained?

- The founding staff continued to work hard themselves and encourage new employees in the unit to be as dedicated.

This Retrospective Journey Map shows that the key turning point in CSS's development was when the staff gave up the illusion they could do it all on their own and discovered they needed help. The group also discovered that CSS relied on a strategy of hard work, conscientiousness, and self-sacrifice. Their key resource was their knowledge of rules, procedures, and ways of achieving things. ◀

▶ Application: Prospective Journey Map

CSS's current stress and discord showed that its past strategies were no longer effective for the current situation. The stress and discord were calls for new paths. The group members looked at what could lie in their future and what they wanted in their future. Here's their sample prospective map.

Inertia—What Will Be Immobilizing the Creative Energy?

- The dominance of the long-service staff and their approaches to managing CSS.

Call—What Will Be Motivating the Creative Energy?

- Meeting the complex challenges of global operations in multiple jurisdictions.

Jump—What Will Be the Unknown?

- The globalization of TCom and its sponsoring company.

Trials—What Will Be the Change Dragons?

- The continuous influx of staff and contract employees from diverse cultures and world regions, combined with the resulting conflict.

Dissolution—What Limiting Pattern Will Have to Be Given Up?

- Current structure and operational philosophy.

Discovery—What New Pattern Will Have to Be Adopted?

- Fast, flexible, and responsive services and harmonious staff relations.

Integration—How Will Synergy Be Created?

- Superior orientation of new employees; creation of a new identity that transcends the division between long-service employees and newcomers.

Application—How Will the New Pattern Be Enacted or Sustained?

- Implement a new vision of CSS as a competent and innovative unit providing superior services to support global operations.

The group discovered through Prospective Journey Mapping that it needed to create a new vision, identity, and operational philosophy to adapt to emerging conditions outside and within TCom. To fine-tune the journey map, group members concluded by creating a continuum map. ◄

► Application: Continuum Map

CSS created a continuum map to bridge the past, present, and future. Group members chose to see themselves as experiencing the Trials Cycle, so the "current" phase was trials.

Inertia—What Was (Past Tense) Immobilizing the Creative Energy?

- The dominant control of the long-service employees and their reliance on hard work and self-sacrifice as operational strategies.

Call—What Was Motivating the Creative Energy?

- The success of TCom's internationalization and the desire to provide good services.

Jump—What Was the Unknown?

- The 500 percent expansion of the unit in under twelve months.

Trials—What Are (Present Tense) the Change Dragons to Be Confronted?

- The fear among long-service employees of losing control, combined with the desire of the newcomers to innovate with new systems and practices without regard for integration, continuity, or acknowledgement of solutions already in place.

Dissolution—What Old Patterns Will (Future Tense) Have to Be Let Go?

- The division between old and new, the culture of us and them. Both the long-service employees and the newcomers have to give up the illusion that they can do it all by themselves. They also have to renounce seeing their own way as the only way.

Discovery—What New Pattern Will Emerge and What New Gifts Will Have to Be Accepted?

- Collaboration between long-service employees and newcomers.
- The emergence of a globally oriented service organization.

Integration—How Will Synergy Be Created?

- The group will explore its commonalities and differences and use these as a platform to introduce new programs and services.

Application—How Will the New Patterns Be Enacted or Sustained?

- CSS will involve its internal and external clients to participate in the change process and act as collaborators and evaluators. ◀

The three applications illustrate that a group can gain clarity and discover direction through variations of the ACJ Questionnaires. By asking the same questions in a different context, the group is prompted to come up with new answers to match the changing environment.

Using the information and guidelines provided about Journey Mapping, practitioners can now apply the ACJ approach in organizations with greater confidence. You may want to start by doing the practice activities for this chapter.

Practice Activities

1. Focus on a client system. Identify the call signals in the organization. What pathfinding systems and techniques can you identify in your client system?

2. Using the ACJ Map framework, create a coherent story of the change journeys occurring in your client system.

3. Create three journey maps for the above client system: retrospective, prospective, and continuum.

4. What are some ways for you to apply Journey Mapping techniques with your clients?

Summary and Preview

Once an organization answers the call to journey, it will seek a new course of change. This chapter looked at the characteristics of the Call Cycle and some key actions in pathfinding. I described the steps in facilitating a Journey Mapping group session. Using these steps, you can work with groups to identify change paths. You learned about three Journey Mapping techniques: retrospective, prospective, and continuum. They give you more options in fine-tuning a change journey. I illustrated the applications of these techniques by using a case situation from TCom.

Once an organization embarks on a new path, its commitment to change will be tested. In the next chapter, we will look at the Jump Cycle. You will learn about TCom HR manager Julee's jump experience and how she, by embracing the unknown, leads her organization into new territory.

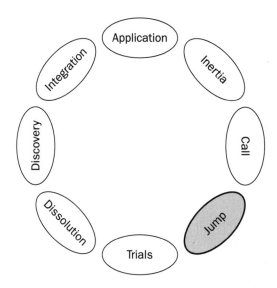

What is the unknown? What new energy is lurking there?

(5)

Jump and Adventuring

THE JUMP CYCLE IS ABOUT making a commitment to change. Jump takes people and organizations into quantum leaps, reaching for an expanded or higher level of awareness and functioning. Wolinsky (1993) refers to quantum jumps as shifts in level of understanding. According to our working Archetypal Change Theory, people and organizations can self-organize their own shifts in awareness and functioning. They can do that when they are in touch with and trust in the change intelligence within and around them. Trust is a critical factor in taking a quantum leap because one is venturing into the unknown. In mythological tales, the unknown usually represents the untapped potential in individuals and society (Campbell & Moyers, 1991). By venturing into the unknown, Archetypal Change Systems can work toward their full development. But how does this working theory play out among people and organizations? This chapter will look at the story of Julee, TCom's HR manager, and her effort to deal with diversity in TCom and TCom's sponsoring organization, Linco. I will describe how Julee responds to the challenges of the Jump Cycle and how her quantum leap is intertwined with the quantum leap of the organizations she works with. Let's begin by discussing the meaning of jump and the practice of adventuring.

Jumping into the Unknown

Jump represents a commitment to traverse the unknown. Jump can be the point of no return in the transformation process. In Chinese mythology, when Sheung-Ngaw hastily drinks a stolen elixir (metaphor for knowledge), she irrevocably commits herself to a higher level of awareness and functioning, in her case as the moon goddess. Similarly, when Icarus, flapping wax-fastened wings, flies too near the sun, he embarks on a journey of no return. You can see, then, that jump represents a dangerous opportunity. There is no knowing what lies at the bottom of the abyss. On the other hand, a jump is what it takes to reap the rewards of change. Jump can be a thrilling experience, too. It moves you out of routine and on to adventures. Five simple practices that can help you embrace the adventure of jumping into the unknown are described below. I call them adventuring practices.

Adventuring Practices

The first practice is *to provide perspectives,* the ability to view a scene from a distance to take in the whole. Change agents can help provide this holistic perspective to the adventure of change. When people see how venturing into the unknown can advance their transformation, they are ready to take on the risk with greater conviction. You can use the Journey Mapping techniques to create a holistic perspective of the eight cycles of change. Later in this chapter, we will look at the Diversity Systems Matrix, which you can use to create a holistic picture of an organization.

The second adventuring practice is *to embrace uncertainty,* which is the state of not knowing how things will unfold. It can be viewed as unrealized potential. As change agents, you can help clients to embrace uncertainty by asking the key questions of the Jump Cycle: "Where is the unknown?" "What new energy is lurking there?"

The third adventuring practice is *to become conscious of prejudices.* Prejudices are prejudgments or biases that limit your perspective and cause you to shut out adventures. To practice adventuring, you want to become conscious of prejudices. You can detect prejudices by identifying the unspoken assumptions behind your thoughts and actions. When you are aware of your assumptions, you can act consciously and intentionally. You can use the de-centering and re-centering technique discussed in Chapter Three to remove prejudices that dominate your world. In the discussion of the Dissolution Cycle, you will learn specific techniques to identify prejudices that limit creativity.

The fourth adventuring practice is *to explore your tolerance to risk.* Jump is risky because the outcome is unpredictable. However, our working Archetypal Change Theory suggests that people and organizations self-organize their own quantum leaps. This means that their own risk tolerance can be the best guide as to whether a jump is doable. Change agents want to respect their clients' risk tolerance. You can help increase risk tolerance by exploring risk and reward tradeoffs. You can also use Retrospective and Prospective Journey Mapping techniques to identify past successful risk taking and anticipate the shape of future risks.

The fifth adventuring practice is *to trust.* Jump is a leap of faith. You can learn to trust by clarifying change intention and purpose. Ask questions such as, "What gives us life and energy in this organization?" and "What's our purpose?" When you are clear about your intention, you can act out of trust. When you act out of trust, you are shaping the leap of faith to take you to a higher level of awareness and functioning.

The above five practices can serve as a checklist when guiding clients to commit to the unknown. The following list can serve as a handy reminder.

Adventuring Practices Checklist

When guiding adventures, I . . .

☐ Provide a holistic perspective to help clients take risk with greater awareness.

☐ Ask key questions of the Jump Cycle to help clients embrace uncertainty.

☐ Help clients identify the unspoken assumptions behind their thoughts and actions to surface limiting prejudices.

☐ Help clients to explore risk and reward tradeoffs.

☐ Respect clients' risk tolerance.

☐ Encourage clients to learn trust by clarifying their own change intention and purpose.

Now, let's look at how Julee deals with the unknown in her practice and in the organizations she works with.

Diversity as Unknown Territory

In my view, for most 21st Century organizations, the unknown is not some uncharted region in the physical world. Rather, the unknown that we want to survey lies in the diversity and complexity of our organizational landscape. Before venturing out to conquer a new frontier, we want first to survey how well we are using the untapped talents of diversity within us. Such a survey will identify changes needed to adapt successfully in the global world. Not surprisingly, many organizations have made efforts to respond to the call of diversity and have initiated change activities (Arrien, 1998). Linco is such an organization.

Linco is a venerable corporation with a diverse workforce. Its business interests encompass transportation, energy, and communication. Like other companies, Linco has instituted diversity training for its employees for several years. Recently, a number of factors have contributed to a renewed interest in diversity among Linco management. First, Linco is no longer an employer of choice due to the rise of high technology and other new economy sectors. Second, Linco's competitors have developed a better reputation for dealing with diversity. Third, executives of TCom, Linco's international arm, have raised the issue of diversity in international business. Linco has decided to conduct a survey to assess its situation. The survey was assigned to Julee, TCom's HR manager.

Julee's Quandary

Julee has mixed feelings about the survey. She is pleased with the assignment, as she had emphasized the importance of diversity when she worked at Linco. On the other hand, she is concerned because she knows diversity is not a popular issue at Linco. She has doubts about her own ability to manage the survey. Julee recognizes that the diversity issue should not be addressed separately from overall organization change. She wonders if she is being set up for failure.

Julee is keenly aware of the tension between Linco and TCom. When TCom was first set up, it was viewed as an out-of-the-way place for out-of-favor employees. With TCom's recent success, Linco employees began to view TCom as an internal competitor, a rebel to be reined in. On the other hand, TCom's new leaders and employees found Linco unaware of what it takes to operate in other countries.

TCom resented what it perceived as time-consuming bureaucratic demands from Linco. Employees like Julee felt caught in the middle.

Jumping Offshore?

When Julee was first assigned to TCom, she was thrilled with the prospect of hands-on international experience. She had looked forward to traveling to offshore locations and embracing the unknown in far-off lands. But it turned out that the unknown she encountered was right in TCom's head office. She had planned to expand her HR function to include organization effectiveness. But she found she was overwhelmed by the heavy workload of fighting fires within the organization. Life in TCom was chaotic as people made up rules and procedures as they went along. Julee grew anxious about the perception that she was more Linco than TCom. In several instances, she was uncomfortable with how some managers dealt with issues, but she bit her tongue and remained silent. One of these issues concerned the coordination of consultants Daryn and Hingram (introduced in earlier chapters). Daryn was sponsored by Linco's CEO, who promoted her leadership and team-building work to all of Linco and its affiliates. Hingram was hired by Arthur Jay, TCom's CEO. Julee saw the need for greater coordination among the different change initiatives. She was unsure of herself and felt increasingly distressed. To seek advice and sometimes to let off steam, Julee found herself drawn back to old relationships in Linco. This behavior was viewed negatively by TCom executives.

Julee's Journey

In Julee's story so far, we see a number of classic change cycles. Julee is called away from the *inertia* at Linco. She answers the *call* to journey with high hopes. Instead of fully jumping off into the unknown of TCom, though, she finds herself drawn back to her old relationships in Linco. But people are telling her that returning to inertia is not tenable. So what must Julee do now? What does Julee want to do? What new energy is lurking in the unknown? What exactly is the unknown for Julee? Let's see how Julee orchestrates her own quantum leap and how this leap can potentially help her organizations move to a different place.

Meeting a Journey Guide

Julee grows concerned about her job security at TCom. To explore new opportunities, she attends an organization development conference, where she meets practitioner Arente. Julee is attracted to Arente's workshop on Archetypal Change

Journeys because the journey idea resonates with her. The Journey Mapping technique helps her to make sense of her career at Linco and TCom. She realizes that when she is unclear about or untrusting of her inner voice, she is weak and fearful. When she acts out of fear, she does not connect with others. Her Journey Mapping (see Figure 5.1) also reveals she is fearful of letting go of familiar thinking and established relationships. This reluctance to let go means she is not able to fully embrace what is new in her work. In her concern for security, she loses touch with what gives her life and joy. In her concern to change others, she forgets to keep up with her own transformation. She becomes disconnected from what drew her into the human resource and organization development field in the first place—to work with people from diverse backgrounds and to use herself as an instrument for change.

Julee finds it ironic that she feels anxious about working with TCom managers and consultants Daryn and Hingram. She had advocated that diversity was a source of synergy, yet she is unable even to connect with those who are different or unfamiliar. Journey Mapping helps Julee recognize that she is intimidated by their differences. The workshop spurs Julee to take stock of her work. By repeatedly mapping her journeys retrospectively and prospectively, she rediscovers her purpose and interest. She decides to make a jump and embrace the unknown in her life without delay. That entails working with diversity and using herself as an instrument of change in TCom and Linco. Julee also decides to invite Arente to work with TCom and help coordinate its multiple changes. To Julee's relief, Arente and his work are well-received. Julee learns that her boss, Arthur Jay, is pleased with her initiative and, in fact, had waited for some time for her to take charge. Similarly, when Julee finally approaches Daryn and Hingram, she also finds them more than happy to collaborate with her on the diversity initiative. The lesson from Julee's journey is that, when Julee acts out of her own change intention, she is able to connect with those around her. Exhibit 5.1 (see page 90) is a worksheet that Julee uses to move from inertia to jump.

Meeting Diversity Challenges

Diversity initiatives by organizations often remain stalled despite significant investment in them. A number of challenges contribute to this inertia. First, diversity is often treated as a side issue or an add-on to satisfy legal requirements or appease internal discontent. Second, people working in diversity issues are often not connected with other change agents in the same organization. The disjointedness makes it difficult for people to know what the real change intention is. Third, diversity is complex. Diversity can refer to differences of race, gender, ethnicity,

Figure 5.1. A Sample from Julee's Journey Maps

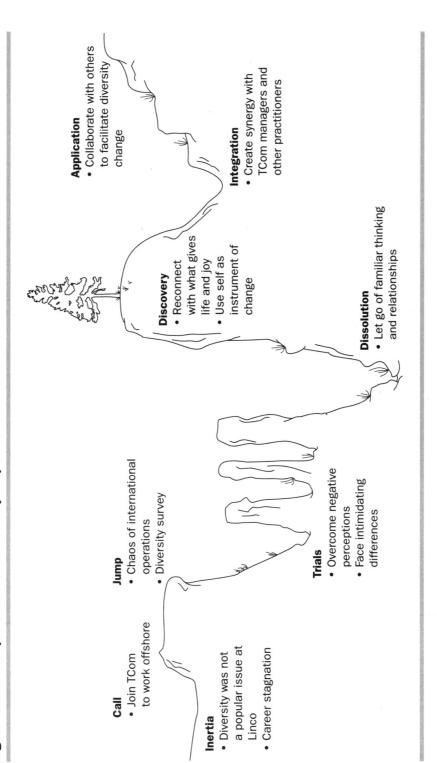

Call
- Join TCom to work offshore

Inertia
- Diversity was not a popular issue at Linco
- Career stagnation

Jump
- Chaos of international operations
- Diversity survey

Trials
- Overcome negative perceptions
- Face intimidating differences

Discovery
- Reconnect with what gives life and joy
- Use self as instrument of change

Dissolution
- Let go of familiar thinking and relationships

Application
- Collaborate with others to facilitate diversity change

Integration
- Create synergy with TCom managers and other practitioners

Adapted in part from *The Hero with a Thousand Faces* by Joseph Campbell (1968). Princeton, NJ: Princeton University Press.

Exhibit 5.1. Moving from Inertia to Jump

The following is a list of questions Julee used to help her make the jump into the unknown. You may find the questions helpful in clarifying your own change journey.

Inertia

What has been making me stuck?

What patterns have I been repeating?

How do these patterns stop me from being creative?

What or who keeps me powerless?

Call

What are the call signals?

What messages have I been ignoring?

What gave me joy in my work?

What gives me joy in my work now?

Is my current job still the right calling for me?

What can I do differently in my work?

Jump

What are my fears?

Who in the organization do I fear? Why?

What could happen to me if I took some risks?

What are these risks?

What could I gain from taking a risk?

age, sexual orientation, nationality, language, religion, abilities, values, beliefs, styles, tenure, rank, job in the organization, and so on. Fourth, understanding diversity is still mostly uncharted territory.

These challenges have also been Linco's experience. Daryn, Hingram, and Arente agree with Julee that diversity is integral to the success of Linco and TCom; it should be part of organization change. To overcome the disjointedness referred to above, Julee and the other practitioners agree to collaborate. To meet the complexity challenge, the change practitioners want to seek new ideas and paradigms that address complexity, such as chaos and complexity science. To lessen the fear of the unknown, the change practitioners want to open eyes to new perspectives and help clients identify the risks and the rewards of diversity change journeys.

The four practitioners come up with a multi-faceted approach to frame the Diversity Survey. First, they outline a contract for management involvement and an organization change emphasis. Second, they agree to use the Diversity Systems Matrix method (Allen, 1999) to conduct the survey. (This matrix will be described shortly.) Third, they plan to involve management in creating a journey map to shape and guide the diversity process. Fourth, they will integrate diversity into other change initiatives, including work offered by Daryn (leadership and team building) and Hingram (relationship coaching). Fifth, they will teach employees to use the Journey Mapping technique to shape and coordinate change journeys. Sixth, the practitioners agree to monitor their own journeys as well as those of the two organizations.

Securing Management Commitment

The practitioners decide that, before making a formal proposal to Linco management, they should sound out individual executive support. They discover that most of Linco's executives view the scope of work as too broad, the process too unpredictable, and the outcome too intangible. However, they do support a survey to be conducted by FR Inc., the consulting firm that handles Linco's organizational climate surveys. A suggestion from Arthur Jay, TCom CEO, then gives them an alternative. Daryn usually does team building with Linco management at the quarterly retreat for senior executives. Arthur Jay agrees to sponsor a session for the practitioners to try out their proposed activities with Linco management. The four practitioners want to invite select employees from different parts of the organization to join the executives. Daryn agrees to brief Tedd Smithe, Linco CEO, on how the diversity plan would support other change initiatives.

In the session, the executives and employees have hands-on experience with the matrix and the Journey Mapping technique and learn about diversity's central importance in organization change. The collaboration of the four practitioners helps to make a coherent case for diversity and the session is well-received. Retreat participants give input to further customize the proposed survey. From Julee's perspective, Linco management's participation in the retreat and their support for the expanded diversity survey is an organizational quantum leap. For herself, the collaboration with the three consultants and her boss, Arthur Jay, is a personal quantum leap.

Intertwining Leaps

We have followed the intertwining journeys of Julee and her organizations. We saw how Julee's call to journey landed her in distress and uncertainty about her relationship to TCom. In despair, she sought help by going to a conference where she met a guide, Arente. By using the intelligence embodied in the Archetypal Change Journey, Julee rediscovered her own forgotten purpose and interest. Her rediscovery led her to embrace the unknown in her organization—dealing with diversity and collaborating with others. The collaboration created new synergies that stimulated new strategies and patterns. Linco management's initial request for a diversity survey was a catalyst in mobilizing Julee and the three practitioners. Once mobilized, Julee and the practitioners returned to challenge Linco management to jump to an expanded level of awareness and functioning. These intertwining quantum leaps are part of the excitement and challenge of embracing the unknown. Now, we will look at the Diversity Systems Matrix and how to use it for assessing the capacity for diversity in organizations.

Diversity Systems Matrix

The Diversity Systems Matrix was inspired by Marlis Buchmann's (1989) work on human development. The matrix surveys the structural, cultural, systemic, and experiential landscapes of an organization. Graphically, the matrix is a square field or box divided into four parts with a circle in the middle. (See Figure 5.2.) The four fields or landscapes represent four basic aspects of an organization. The circle in the middle represents the system under focus—in this case Linco and TCom. The dividing lines are dotted, implying that the divisions are fluid and quite arbitrary. The fields are interconnected and mutually influencing.

Figure 5.2. Diversity Systems Matrix

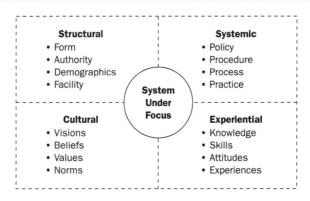

The following describes what each field surveys.

Field 1 gathers information on the *structural* landscape of an organization. Structures—like pillars and beams—shape the flow of creative exchange in organizations. They create opportunities, but also set limits. The structural landscape of an organization includes demographic characteristics and ranking distribution, organizational form (hierarchy, self-directed teams), communication flow, technologies, and physical facilities. The key question is "Do the structures of the organization enhance or block diversity and creativity?"

Field 2 gathers information about the *cultural* landscape of an organization. *Material culture* refers to tangible things, such as products, logos, annual reports, and office decor. *Symbolic culture* refers to preferences about what is important (values), expectations about what behavior is appropriate (norms), and assumptions about what is real about the world and people (worldviews). The cultural landscape thus includes vision, values, beliefs, worldviews, language, norms, customs, and rituals. The key question is "Does the culture value or deprecate diversity in this organization?"

Field 3 gathers information about systemic *processes, practices, policies,* or *procedures* that guide the business and its employment activities. The systemic landscape includes business systems (such as research, production, marketing, finance, partnerships, and investor relations) and employment systems (such as hiring, compensation, promotion, termination, training, and education). The key question is "Do policies, practices, and procedures support or block the value of diversity in the organization?"

Field 4 gathers information about the *experiential* or *individual* landscape, the thoughts, feelings, and behavior participants acquire from working in the organization. This field also includes special knowledge, skills, and attitudes, the competencies required for productivity in an organization. The experiential landscape gives life to an organization. Without individuals, there would be no structures, cultures, and systems.

The four fields are mutually influencing and regulate the flow of creativity within an organization. The interaction of these fields creates special patterns and matrices of self-organization. For example, the pattern of hierarchy is created by hierarchical structures, cultures, systems, and experiences. To produce a network pattern, you need network structure, culture, systems, and experiences. Because the fields are interlinked, you can start your change intervention in any field, provided that you continue to work through all the fields, in order to bring about systemic change. Systemic change means changing the pattern of the whole organization. As a result, for organizations such as Linco to benefit from diversity, they have to go beyond diversity training to making systemic changes to their organizational landscape. These points can be brought home when participants create their own Diversity Systems Matrices.

Although this explanation of the matrix may sound complicated, in practice, it is quite easy to use. I have guided hundreds of people, at all levels of various organizations, to use this matrix to assess their own organizations. Following is an instructional script you can adapt.

Instructional Script for Using the Matrix

"I want to first explain the purpose of the matrix. It is a simple tool to help you assess your own organization's diversity capacity. It is important to have your own understanding, because ultimately you will determine the success or failure of your diversity initiative.

"There are four interrelated fields of assessment, which will create a whole picture of the organization. These fields are structural, cultural, systemic, and experiential/individual. This graph [show Figure 5.2] shows the kind of information to look for in each field.

"In the *structural* field (Field 1), try to identify the form of the organization. For example, most organizations have a hierarchical structure of different ranks [draw a pyramid with ranks]. On the top rank, you may find group A, in the second tier, you may find group B, and so on. Some groups are not represented in the organization. How is this hierarchical structure supported or sustained?

"Let's look at the next field, the *cultural* field (Field 2). What kind of values and norms are key in this organization? In what ways do they reinforce and support existing structure?

"Next, we look at the *systemic* field (Field 3)—the policies, processes, practices, and procedures that guide everyday actions in the organization. For example, how do recruitment policies and practices support existing structure and cultural values and norms?

"Last, we look at the *experiential* field (Field 4). How do individuals within the organization experience it? What knowledge, skills, and attitudes do they have to support the organization? Are they able to exercise their creative talents? What are their peak and pit experiences?

"For diversity to be valued and supported, we need all four fields to work together. Without the support of structures, cultures, and systemic practices, individual valuing of diversity will not be sufficient. This may explain why diversity change agents frequently burn out before completing their objectives. Having the right policies and procedures while missing the cultural and individual support will also be insufficient. By obtaining information in all four fields, you will have a clearer idea of your organization's diversity capacity.

"Now, I invite you to work in small groups to create a Diversity Systems Matrix for your organization. Here is a matrix worksheet. [Hand out a copy of Exhibit 5.2 to each small group.] In the center circle, write the name of your organization or unit. Then share your experiences and observations regarding each of the four fields. Do not be too concerned about putting the right information in the right fields; they are all interconnected. Focus on creating a whole picture. Once all groups have completed their matrices, we'll come together and share them. Then, the next task will be to create a new matrix of change by identifying key change actions in each of the four fields."

Exhibit 5.2. Diversity Systems Matrix Worksheet

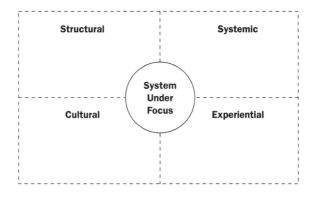

Following are some additional guidelines for using the Diversity Systems Matrix.

Guidelines on Using the Diversity Systems Matrix

- Label the center circle of the matrix form with the system you want to focus on. The system can be an enterprise, a division, or a small group.

- Using the fields as a focusing lens, bring participants' experiences and observations to the surface. You can work on all fields simultaneously or sequentially. Keep an open mind.

- Pay attention to your intuition and internal sensor. Let the data sit. Talk about your discoveries.

- The survey can be done individually, in small groups, or in a large assembly. Try to have a diversity of ranks, backgrounds, and jobs in your groups.

▶ Application: Linco's Diversity Systems Matrix

In the course of the diversity survey at Linco, many Diversity Systems Matrices were created. An abbreviated sample follows:

- *Field 1, the Structural Landscape:* Linco's dominant structure is a hierarchy with semi-autonomous business units. Linco has a large diverse workforce. Demographic diversity is represented in the lower and middle ranks. In particular, a high percentage of women was found in the lowest ranks of the organization. Mostly white men populate the senior management ranks. There were attempts to hire more women into senior ranks, but a number of them left after staying less than a five-year period.

- *Field 2, the Cultural Landscape:* Linco's corporate culture has a mix of arrow and spiral characteristics, with the arrow perspective accepted as the driving force. Aggression and relentlessness are highly valued. Fast execution of strategies is viewed as critical to high performance. Thinking, creativity, and collaboration are espoused but, in practice, not highly regarded. This means that, despite the presence of cultural diversity, the range of behavior that is actually valued is quite narrow. Another cultural feature is the lack of success in fostering an environment of respect for professional women. Due to the high concentration of women in the lower ranks, men and women in the organization are used to seeing women as assistants. People of color also experience difficulty in being viewed as potential executive leaders. In short, stereotyping still persists in Linco's cultural landscape.

- *Field 3, the Systemic Landscape:* Linco has difficulty in becoming an employer of choice. Recent drives to promote team practices and empowered decision making have modified the traditional hierarchical processes and created some openness. However, micromanagement and red tape still dominate. Employees who want to innovate have to do it covertly.

- *Field 4, the Experiential Landscape:* Linco employees are loyal and devoted to the company. Many have been there for years. They are adept at responding to crises. As Linco was originally founded as a high-technology company, many of its employees are attuned to innovation and creativity. Many employees bring multicultural and multilingual capabilities, but the organization does not tap into these skills.

The above matrix shows that there was considerable diversity within Linco, but the diversity was not consciously valued or converted into a competitive advantage. Linco's current matrix was better geared to producing homogeneity. The matrix method helped Linco to reconnect to its origin as an innovative high-technology company. It provided a framework for conversations about regenerating Linco's inventive spirit and the development of diversity to help Linco make the jump into the 21st Century. ◀

Linco is a long-established company. For contrast, let's look at a matrix application to a high-tech startup called KodeCo.

► Application: Jump into the Big League?

Nadir, Suu, and Lee are technology enthusiasts who developed an encryption product that they wanted to market. An initial round of private financing enabled them to start a small operation, KodeCo. Product and venture-capital interest soared when a spate of security breaches hit the press. KodeCo was poised for the next level. How should KodeCo manage the jump? What would KodeCo's go-forward landscape and strategy look like? Here are the findings from KodeCo's matrix survey:

- *Field 1, the Structural Landscape:* KodeCo was founded on the three partners' passion for technology. To develop as an enterprise, KodeCo needs other supporting pillars, namely financial, marketing, and operation. The three partners have to welcome and include new talents in their business.

- *Field 2, the Cultural Landscape:* KodeCo's culture reflects the values and habits of the three partners: intense technology focus, informality, and aversion to administration. As more employees and stakeholders become involved, KodeCo needs to diversify its culture to include newcomers' values, preferences, and styles. The three partners have to overcome their prejudices about people whose expertise lies outside of technology.

- *Field 3, the Systemic Landscape:* As the partners are good friends as well as colleagues, decision making is part of their daily interaction. To make the next level, KodeCo needs to develop more formal and systematic policies, procedures, and processes to deal with burgeoning needs in recruitment, marketing, customer and investor relations, and financial management.

- *Field 4, the Experiential Landscape:* KodeCo's founding expertise was encryption technology. To go further, KodeCo wants to add business knowledge, skills, and experience. Their motivation must expand beyond technological innovation to creating a credible business model with a compelling story for potential clients. Emotionally, the original partners and other stakeholders want to come to terms with the leap—high tech is high risk. The next jump can be the thrill of a lifetime or it can be a headlong dash to failure. ◄

KodeCo follows a familiar developmental path for high-tech firms. Although the path is well-known, it is nonetheless new to the KodeCo stakeholders. The matrix process provides a disciplined way to explore this critical juncture in their journey.

Practice Activities

1. Survey and identify the unknown in your organization. What new energy is lurking there?

2. What is the state of diversity in your organization? What role does it play in organization change? How do change agents work together?

3. Create a Diversity Systems Matrix for your organization. Does it support or inhibit the development of your organization's diversity capacity? Show how you might remove any barriers to the development of your organization's diversity capacity by identifying a key action in each of the four fields.

4. What are some of the unknown issues in your own practice as a change agent? How do you incorporate uncertainty into your work in organizations?

Summary and Preview

This chapter followed the intertwining journeys of Julee and her companies, Linco and TCom. Julee's story illustrates how people and organizations can self-orchestrate their own leaps to an expanded level of awareness and functioning. The context for Julee's journey was exploring organizational diversity. Examples of the Diversity Systems Matrix method for surveying diversity capacity in organizations were provided.

Diversity change is uncharted territory for most organizations. This territory can be a place inhabited by change dragons that distract people from their change intention and derail change efforts. Instead of leaping to higher levels of awareness and functioning, people can become trapped in greed, victimization, and lethargy. Dealing with change dragons is the focus of the next chapter.

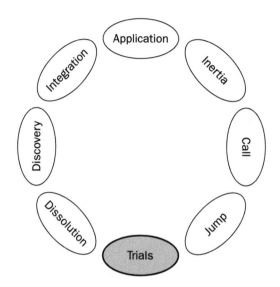

What are the change dragons you must confront?

6

Trials and Dancing with Dragons

ON THE TRANSFORMATION JOURNEY, there can be many obstacles that distract from change intention and derail change efforts. I call these obstacles *change dragons.* Confronting change dragons is the challenge of the Trials Cycle in the Archetypal Change Journey. This confrontation is described as "dancing with dragons."

To help you learn more about dancing with dragons, I will introduce the Lotus Path Method from the Hindu-Buddhist tradition (Campbell, 1986, 1990). The Lotus Path will teach you about seven archetypal change energies and their manifestations in organizations. In this chapter, I will focus on three of them. The Lotus Path brings three important benefits to the Trials Cycle of the Archetypal Change Journey. First, it helps you name the change dragons, which is a key step in dancing with dragons. Second, it identifies the polar experiences associated with the change dragons: fears and desires. Third, it shows you healthy change energies to keep you on track. You start by learning more about trials and dancing with dragons.

Facing Trials

Trials are challenging situations, either initiated from within or imposed from without. A self-initiated restructuring or a plunge in share price may trigger a period of trials for an organization. In mythological tales, trials represent the "belly-of-the-beast" phase. The heroes and heroines encounter fantastic creatures of all shapes and sizes. Some appear as helpful guides and come bearing gifts. The guides and gifts are manifestations of the blissful aspect of the creative energy. Other creatures assume the form of scary monsters that are the wrathful manifestations of the creative energy (Campbell, 1990). Jonah's adventures with the whale, the daunting tasks of Hercules, St. George's dragon, or the three tests faced by Jesus and Buddha are examples of trials. Confronting both the blissful and wrathful energies arising from them is part of the Trials Cycle.

In the Trials Cycle, a system's energies are cut loose from their customary moorings. These ambient energies can be forces for both chaos and order or, in Dee Hock's (1998) terminology, "chaords." They are processes of self-organization and self-disorganization. I prefer to call these energies "change dragons" or "dragons of change." These dragons can manifest themselves as an organizational feeding frenzy (the indiscriminate abuse of resources), lethargy, aggression, and greed.

Trials prepare a system for the demise of its old form. They contain a bifurcation process that is the turning point in transformation. I will touch on that later.

Organizations are tested physically, structurally, culturally, and emotionally in the Trials Cycle. People are at once delighted and disgusted with what they discover in the underbelly of their systems. Resources will be stretched to their limits. At times, people will attempt to fight to retain control; at other times, they are ready to surrender. They can experience a variety of extreme emotions: despair, anger, envy, denial, and disorientation. In the end, people may be exhausted. All the energies in the system are dissipated. Recognize this experience as the crucible of transformation.

The Trials Cycle opens the proverbial can of worms. As a result, change initiatives are often killed off at this critical period. Projects are shelved; work is discarded. No matter how much investment has already been made, the system feels safer pulling back rather than going forward. Of course, the pulling back is only a postponement of needed change. Before long, the pressure to change will build, and the system will repeat the cycle once more. To be adept at guiding a system through the Trials Cycle, change agents want to be able to dance with the dragons of change.

Dancing with Dragons

Dancing with dragons refers to working with chaordic energies. Dragons are awesome creatures in mythology. In Western mythology, dragons are symbols for demons and monsters to be killed. In the East, they represent vitality and are prized (Campbell & Moyers, 1991). In this book, attempting to bridge Western and Eastern cultures, dragons will be used to symbolize the simultaneous presence of danger and opportunity that a system must face or seize in the course of transformation. Dragons are chaos *and* order. The goal of dancing with dragons is to couple chaos and order so as to bring about the emergence of a more adaptable system. The four core steps in dancing with dragons are described below.

1. Recognize the Dragons' Archetypal Forms. As dragons don many masks and assume many guises, change agents must learn to recognize the dragons' archetypal forms. According to the Lotus Path, the three archetypal dragons are related to consuming (food), relations (fame), and power (fortune).

2. Name the Dragon Fears. It is important to name the fears that drive change in a system. Fear is conscious or unconscious dread that attack, ambush, or other dangers are imminent. The fear of death, rejection, or other pain can generate powerful energies within a system. When a system is not centered, aware, or mindful, it can be frightened by its own energies, just as you may be spooked by a nightmare. Although you are the author of your own dreams—they are the product of your own mind, after all—you may be frightened by them. Fears percolate and circulate throughout human systems in transformation. They can become underground currents directing change covertly. Helping a system to make explicit some of the fears is a way to tap into these volatile energies.

3. Name the Dragon Desires. You must name the desires that drive change in your particular system. The desires, the polar opposite to the fears just discussed, are conscious or unconscious longing or wishing. Like fears, desires can generate enormous energies within a system. These energies can be harnessed to effect transformation. Naming some of the unspoken desires can release you from their grip.

4. Walk Between Fears and Desires. To name the fears and desires is to walk in step with them. As though in a dance, the fear energy pulls you to one side and the desire energy to another. Fears and desires are polarities that draw a system to the extremes. When they are named, as in Steps 2 and 3, the center opens up, providing a void, a space filled with creative tension through which authentic intention can rise (Peat, 1991). The space between a system's fears and desires is the bifurcation point. It is a point at which the system can go either way: The familiar way of fears and desires or a unique and still-unknown middle track. An apt mythological image is the parting of the seas, as in the Jewish Exodus story: Beset by fears and desires on all sides, the Jewish people are able to follow a clear, uncluttered middle course through the divided waters.

Walking through fears and desires or any other pairs of opposites is, I believe, the foundational idea of Confucian wisdom. It signifies the Golden Mean and the Buddhist path of enlightenment. Myths and legends commonly celebrate this walking through the middle—heroic figures making their way past two menacing beasts or heroic voyagers sailing between two giant, crushing rocks. The passage between the rocks opens for a second and, to sail through, you must be focused, precise, and alert.

Using the above four steps gives you greater confidence while working with conflicting energies and emotions. To help you know more about change dragons, let's examine the Lotus Path method.

The Lotus Path Method

The Lotus Path is based on Hindu-Buddhist Kundalini or Chakras systems. My description is, in part, inspired by Joseph Campbell's (1986, 1989, 1990) insights. As a practitioner, I work with human energies. Campbell's interpretations of the Kundalini deepen my understanding of how people and organizations—Archetypal Change Systems—use their energies to orchestrate transformation.

The Lotus Path consists of seven lotuses or energy centers. The seven energy centers are as follows:

Lotus 1: Consuming energy concerned with biological well-being.

Lotus 2: Relational energy concerned with affiliation and legacy.

Lotus 3: Power energy concerned with achievement, competence, and wealth.

Lotus 4: Awakening energy concerned with compassion.

Lotus 5: Radiance energy concerned with spiritual work or enlightenment.

Lotus 6: Rapture energy concerned with joyful identification with the divinity in all creation.

Lotus 7: Bliss energy concerned with unity and transcendence.

These centers help you achieve your creative intentions. The lotuses can self-organize health and well-being. However, they are susceptible to self-disorganization. When the energy centers are self-organizing, a system enjoys health and well-being. When the energy centers are self-disorganizing, the system experiences distortions, blocks, and pain. Because energy centers are mutually influential, there is always unpredictability in transformation. However, through awareness, each system can influence the flow of energy within itself and in the larger systems.

The seven centers can be grouped into two major domains—the biosphere (Lotuses 1, 2, 3) and the spirit sphere (Lotuses 5, 6, 7). Lotus 4, the heart lotus, serves as the bridging link or portal. In this chapter, we will look at the first three lotuses and their change dragons. Chapter Seven will focus on using the heart energies (Lotus 4) for the practice of compassion. In Chapter Eight, you will learn about the transformative power of the upper three lotuses. Figure 6.1 lists the seven lotuses and the nature of their energies.

Now we look at Lotuses 1, 2, and 3 and the fears and desires associated with each of them.

Lotus 1: Consuming Dragon

The essence of Lotus 1 is well-being, aliveness, and health. This energy center is concerned with physical survival. To stay alive, a system has to consume energy. It is in a constant exchange with its environment. For human beings to stay alive, they have to consume air, water, plants, and, in most cases, animals. We also consume ideas, relationships, and emotions. When this energy center is in full form, systems experience the sheer exhilaration of being alive. However, fears and desires can distort the energy. The guises of fears and desires commonly associated with consuming are described below.

First is the *fear of annihilation.* When you are gripped by this fear, you feel that life and survival are at stake, that people and the environment are threatening your safety. You cannot relax and enjoy life. You must be in a state of constant vigilance, looking out for danger and enemies.

Figure 6.1. The Lotus Path

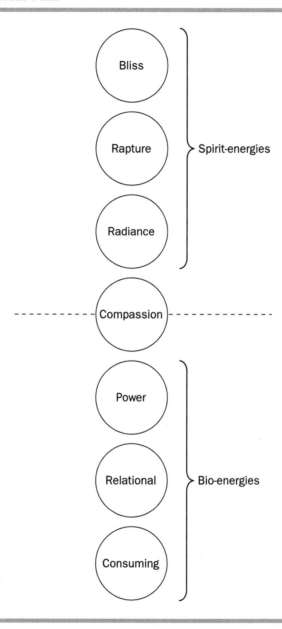

Adapted in part from J. Campbell (1989), *The World of Joseph Campbell: Transformations of Myth Through Time.* A production of William Free Productions, Mythology Limited, and Holoform Research Inc. Chicago, IL: Public Media Video.

Second is the *fear caused by envy*. When you compare yourself with others and their life's rewards, you find you come up short. There is a constant feeling of lacking or being deprived in relation to others. In this mode, you never feel satisfied because, no matter how much you have, there are always others with more.

Third is the *fear arising from lethargy*. What life has to offer neither motivates nor interests you. The change energy is stagnant and is barely alive. You repeat the same mindless patterns and function as though on automatic pilot.

Now we turn to the desires within the Consuming Dragon. Its energy can first be distracted by numerous desires to possess and hoard, resulting from the fear of deprivation. In organizations, *hoarding* can manifest itself in acquisition binges: Buying up businesses without regard to core intent. Hoarding is not restricted to material things. It applies to people, contacts, relationships, affection, and energy.

Another desire leads to what I call the *feeding frenzy* or the compulsion to consume. People apply energy indiscriminately, gripped by the urge to gobble up food, material things, relationships, and whatever else is available. This desire is characterized by high-energy output—mindless consumption is combined with aggressive competition.

A third desire is *greed*, the push to acquire and possess more than is needed or more than contributes to a system's well-being. One craves excess. It can trigger an overwhelming wish to have what actually doesn't belong to you.

Lotus 2. Relational Dragon

Concerned with relationships and legacy, the Relational Dragon is based in the reproductive instinct, but goes beyond biological replication to include all affiliational or pairing concerns. The goal is to be attractive and appealing to others in order to be deemed acceptable, adequate, and, most of all, loved, whether as a leader, corporate citizen, innovator, or successful member of a network. The essence of Lotus 2 is a sense of belonging or being part of something bigger than oneself. This translates into a concern to create a legacy, to leave something of oneself behind. When the energy center is functioning properly, a system experiences the joys and sorrows of full participation in human community.

However, relational energies can be distorted by the following fears. First is the *fear of rejection*, based on the belief one is not quite good enough compared to others. One can be filled with self-doubt and low self-esteem. Others are estimated to be better, richer, or smarter. They also have standards that you cannot possibly meet. Unforgiving criticism and demand for perfection are other manifestations of this fear.

Second is the *fear of abandonment.* This is the anxiety that others, especially those you count on or depend on, will forsake you. To forestall being abandoned or betrayed, you may distance yourselves from others, withhold your trust, and generally live in anticipation of desertion.

Desires can also distort the relational energies of Lotus 2. One desire is *lust* or a strong need for gratification of the senses. Lust can manifest itself as overindulgence in food, relationships, money, rewards, image, and particular mindsets or routines. In organizations, lust shows up as the desire for approval, acceptance, adoration, bigger salaries, more stock options, more impressive titles, or bigger offices.

Another distracting desire in Lotus 2 is based on *seduction.* This is a compulsion to attract and entice others to partner or affiliate with you. The enticement may be based on deception or trickery. The underlying motivation may be fear of rejection, conceit, or vanity. Instead of honest relationships with customers and suppliers, corporations use trickery or deceptive means. Gimmicky marketing may be used instead of the honest description of products.

Lotus 3. Power Dragon

Focused on achievement, wealth, and power, the aim of Lotus 3 is social success and a sense of efficacy. In organizations, the Power Dragon manifests itself in the drive to set goals, meet targets, and surpass expectations. The system wants to be in control of itself and its environment. It wants to harness available economic and psycho-social resources to establish a distinct identity and presence in the world. The maximization of ego distinctiveness goes hand in hand with status achievement. In short, Lotus 3 is about the will to create and having the confidence and resources to get things done.

When Lotus 3 is functioning properly, the system experiences competence and power. It is skillful and resourceful. It achieves goals and is well-recognized and rewarded by society. But if this center is blocked, the system can become preoccupied with *defeat, victimhood, conquest, aggression,* and *hate.*

Defeat is related to a sense of impending setback, failure, or loss of control. You imagine that others are strong, powerful, and in control and you are afraid of being beaten or humiliated. When a human system is gripped by the fear of defeat, it loses confidence and the willingness to take risk. Self-doubt and feelings of powerlessness may prevail.

A second fear is *victimhood.* You feel that others are out to take advantage of you and treat you in unfair or unjust ways. You are suspicious of other people's motives and doubtful of their integrity. When victimhood pervades a system, its participants may feel they are walking on eggshells. They find it difficult to trust others because they don't want to be hurt. Behind every move lurks an aggressor who is ready to inflict pain.

One desire of the Power Dragon is *aggression.* This is an overcompensation against the fear of defeat. The system feels it has to strike out first. It must take action to forestall attacks from others. A system motivated by aggressive energy can become preoccupied with offensive strategies. Instead of referencing themselves as a source of initiative, aggressive systems center their thinking and orientation on their opponents' real or imagined moves.

A second desire is *conquest.* The world is a place to compete, where the rewards and spoils of conquest go to the strong and powerful. It is inspired by the thrill of winning and acquiring, especially when it is at the expense of others.

Malice—discriminatory action fueled by intense aversion—forms another desire. Through malice, a system exercises the power of hate. Malice is a distorted way to experience aliveness, autonomy, and power.

These energies are powerful catalysts or inhibitors of change. Recognizing these energies in your system and in yourself is a starting point for healthy change. Embracing them and learning to dance with them can increase your success with transformation. In the next section, we will examine several ways of using these concepts in organizations.

Table 6.1 is a summary of the change dragons and their fears and desires. The center column summarizes the healthy expressions of the energy. The fears column summarizes the passive expression of the energy. The desires column summarizes the aggressive expressions of the energy. This chart should be read from the bottom up, beginning with the consuming dragon, as a key aim of the Lotus Path is moving the creative energy from the bottom of the path (Lotus 1) to the top (Lotus 7).

Table 6.1. Dragon Chart

Dragon Fears	Healthy Dragons	Dragon Desires
• Defeat • Victimhood	**Power Dragon** • Resourcefulness • Competence • Authentic realization	• Aggression • Conquest • Malice
• Rejection • Abandonment	**Relational Dragon** • Partnership • Collaboration • Community	• Lust • Seduction
• Annihilation • Envy • Lethargy	**Consuming Dragon** • Well-being • Aliveness • Health	• Hoarding • Feeding frenzy • Greed

For a quick illustration of the use of the Lotus Path, we can go back to HR manager Julee's fears and her confrontation with trials in her organizations, TCom and Linco.

► Application: Julee's Dragons

Julee's concerns with job security were related to the Consuming Dragon; that is, if she were to lose her job, she would have to worry about economic survival. Julee found some TCom managers and consultants intimidating. This had to do with the Relational Dragon—she wanted to work with people from diverse backgrounds but was intimidated by others' differences. Third, she was concerned about her inability to contribute to strategic change. This concern was related to the Power Dragon. She felt she had not exercised her competence as a change agent. ◄

The concerns with food, fame, and fortune have been an integral part of my own journey as an independent consultant. Like Julee, when I am in the grip of these change dragons, I am both stressed and ineffective. It was my own concerns and fascination with how these dragons affect the creative energy in people and organizations that drew me to a deeper investigation of archetypal change. I discovered that confronting fears and desires is a universal pattern in transformation.

The Lotus Path can be adapted into many practical tools. In the following section, we will examine several versions and some case illustrations. The first is a questionnaire.

Dragon Quiz

The Dragon Quiz (Exhibit 6.1) is designed to elicit information about chaordic energies and to prompt creative thinking. Use the Dragon Quiz when your organization seems to be under stress and people are fighting with or taking flight from change. Sometimes, you can loosen the grip of the fears and desires we discussed earlier by just naming them.

Exhibit 6.1. Dragon Quiz

Consuming Dragon

- Name the consuming fears that are at play in the system under study. How do these fears block or facilitate the system's survival?

- Name the consuming desires in the system. How do these desires facilitate or block the system's survival?

- What are some creative and sustainable ways for the system to stay alive and thrive?

Relational Dragon

- Name the relational fears that are at play in the system. How do these fears facilitate or block the system's relationships within and without?

- Name the relational desires in the system. How do these desires facilitate or block the system's relationships within and without?

- What are some creative and sustainable ways for the system to satisfy its relational needs?

Exhibit 6.1. Dragon Quiz, Cont'd

Power Dragon

· Name the power fears that are at play in the system. How do these fears facilitate or block the system's authentic transformation?

· Name the power desires in the system. How do these desires facilitate or block the system's authentic transformation?

· What are some creative and sustainable ways for the system to exercise its power and achieve its goals?

▶ Application: Dragon Quiz Example

Let's apply the Dragon Quiz to Julee's case. At the level of the Consuming Dragon, Julee's creative energy was distorted by the consuming fear of annihilation (loss of livelihood) and the consuming desire of feeding frenzy (applying energy indiscriminately). She could harness the consuming energies by focusing on her reason for being a change agent—to bring health and well-being to herself and her organization.

At the level of the Relational Dragon, Julee's creative energy was distorted by the relational fear of rejection (by company leaders and consultants Daryn and Hingram) and the relational desire for adoration (by the company leaders and consultants). She could harness her relational energies by focusing on her motivation to create synergy with people from diverse backgrounds.

At the level of the Power Dragon, Julee's creative energy was distorted by the power fear of victimization (being set up for failure) and the power desire of conquest (being one up on management and the consultants). She could harness her power energies by focusing on her intent to exercise her competence and talents by serving as an instrument for change. ◀

The Dragon Quiz is an easy way to use the Lotus Path method. Once you become familiar with the Lotus Path, you can adapt it to meet your clients' needs. The next application is a variation on the same theme.

Integrating the Dragons

Integrating the Dragons is a chart (see Exhibit 6.2) for identifying the fears and desires within each Lotus and for finding ways of balancing them for the proper functioning of the three dragon centers. This chart can be used individually and in large or small groups.

Exhibit 6.2. Integrating the Dragons

Instructions: Assume a relaxed state and focus on the system in question. In a detached manner, name the fears and desires as explained earlier. Focus on each fear and desire, and ask what energy can bring it to the center. Name that energy/strategy. Repeat the process with each fear and desire. Specific steps follow:

Step 1: In the left-hand column, name your Power Dragon fears.

Step 2: In the right-hand column, name your Power Dragon desires.

Step 3: In the middle column, identify a centering action or perspective that is based neither on fears nor on desires.

Repeat the same steps for the Relational Dragons and Power Dragons.

System Under Focus: _____

Dragon Fears	Integrate Fears and Desires	Dragon Desires
Power Fears	Power Dragon	Power Desires
Relational Fears	Relational Dragon	Relational Desires
Consuming Fears	Consuming Dragon	Consuming Desires

► Case Study: KodeCo's Trials

After twenty-four months of hard work, KodeCo, a high-technology company, finally went public. Its initial public offering (IPO) attracted a lot of retail investors, and its stock price tripled. The partners, employees, and other stakeholders were elated. In fact, they were quite shocked by their sudden wealth and the high valuation of the firm. There was also pressure to produce. Twelve months after KodeCo's debut, things started to unravel. KodeCo's stock valuation was halved during a market pullback. Its stock supporters seemed to evaporate, and its stock price languished, even during market rallies. Partners and employees began to waver. Fatigue set in. Suddenly, KodeCo became a different sort of organization. Integrating the Dragons could help KodeCo make sense of these phenomena. ◄

Exhibit 6.3 shows KodeCo's attempt to integrate its dragons.

Exhibit 6.3. Integrating KodeCo's Dragons

Dragon Fears	Integrate Fears and Desires	Dragon Desires
Power Fears • Fear of being beaten by competitors • Fear of technical expertise becoming obsolete	**Power Dragon** • Make genuine contribution to the technological revolution • Exercise the power of creativity • Create new value	**Power Desires** • Preoccupied with acquiring other companies • Obsessed with being number one
Relational Fears • Fear of being abandoned by venture capitalists • Fear of customer rejection	**Relational Dragon** • Pride of seeing creativity coming into fruition • Pride of seeing product adopted and used	**Relational Desires** • Impress investors with unrealistic goals • Appetite for praise
Consuming Fears • Stress and burnout • Pessimism about imminent demise	**Consuming Dragon** • Feel alive being part of high-tech revolution • Relish opportunity to create	**Consuming Desires** • Feeding frenzy for quick fixes • Wanting share price to go up

Down the Pit

There is yet another variation of the Lotus Path Method that I call "Down the Pit." This tool (Exhibit 6.4) is designed to pinpoint change dragons and strategies for harnessing both the facilitating and blocking aspects of change dragons. This instrument can be used by individuals and small or large groups. A case illustration of how you can use Down the Pit follows.

Exhibit 6.4. Down the Pit Chart

Instructions: To begin this exercise, create a supportive climate. Focus on a specific change process or initiative in your organization. Brainstorm a list of consuming, relational, and power concerns/issues. Select the key concern/issue from consuming, relational, and power lists to work on. Use the chart below as a template and fill in the cells with your data. Tinker with the data until you come up with some creative strategies.

The specific steps follow. Start with the Consuming Dragon:

Step 1. In column 1, identify the key consuming concern or issue in your system for each of the three dragons.

Step 2. In column 2, identify how this concern/issue facilitates or helps positive change.

Step 3. In column 3, identify how this concern/issue blocks or hinders positive change.

Step 4. In column 4, come up with a strategy that can integrate the facilitating and blocking aspects of the concern/issue. Repeat the same steps for the Relational Dragon and the Power Dragon.

Dragons Under Focus	Facilitating Aspects	Blocking Aspects	Dragon-Taming Strategies
Power Dragon			
Relational Dragon			
Consuming Dragon			

▶ Case: ABCO

ABCO's small HR unit had been expanded to become a department as part of an overall restructuring. The departmental mission was strategic partnership with the other business units. The HR staff worked hard, but their commitment faltered. ◀

ABCO's effort at confronting its dragons is shown in Exhibit 6.5.

Exhibit 6.5. Sample Down the Pit Chart

Dragons Under Focus	Facilitating Aspects	Blocking Aspects	Dragon-Taming Strategies
Power Dragon: Organization stereotypes of HR people	Opportunity to explore assumptions and roles Desire to break out of mold	Fear of knowing unpleasant truths Fear of change Lack skills to change	Survey stereotypes Identify what keeps these stereotypes in place Innovate new roles and behavior Confront stereotyping behavior
Relational Dragon: HR not valued by executive team	Need to be valued Desire to make contribution Interest in learning	The need for external valuation blocks internal creativity and risk taking	De-center importance of executive team Re-center HR unit in the system Focus on service
Consuming Dragon: Unsupportive VP of HR	Untapped leadership Opportunity for distributed leadership Desire to contribute to ABCO's success	Fear of VP sustains collusion Fear of taking leadership Fear of being outsourced	Demand responsibility and performance from VP Confront VP behavior Demonstrate HR's strategic value

We have seen several different formats of the Lotus Path Method and ways of dancing with dragons. Below are some further tips on using the Lotus Path.

Lotus Path Tips

- Present the Archetypal Change Journey as a context.

- Reinforce that the three dragons are universal energies of change. They are both perennial catalysts and inhibitors of transformation.

- As fears and desires are powerful emotions, change agents should apply the Lotus Path method to themselves before using the techniques with others.

Trials and dancing with dragons is an important part of guiding change journeys. The following activities can provide you with some hands-on practice.

Practice Activities

1. What are your experiences with trials? What creative strategies do you use to deal with change obstacles?

2. Identify a change obstacle or concern in your organization. Decide what the archetypal form of the change dragon is: consuming, relational, or power. Name the fears. Name the desires. Brainstorm a creative strategy that arises from neither fear nor desire.

3. Fill out the Dragon Check-Up Chart in Exhibit 6.6.

Exhibit 6.6. Dragon Check-Up Chart

Instructions: List the three dragons and their respective fears and desires. For each fear/desire, indicate in the yes/no column whether or not it exists in your organization or practice. If yes, then provide an example.

Fears/Desires	Yes/No	Examples
Consuming Dragon		
Fear of Annihilation		
Envy		
Lethargy		
Hoarding		
Feeding Frenzy		
Greed		
Relational Dragon		
Fear of Rejection		
Fear of Abandonment		
Lust		
Seduction		
Power Dragon		
Defeat		
Victimhood		
Aggression		
Conquest		
Malice		

Summary and Preview

In this chapter, I described the key characteristics of the Trials Cycle and the four steps in dancing with dragons. I presented the Lotus Path Method and its practical applications for working with change dragons that can distract from creative intentions and derail change efforts. These change dragons are associated with consuming, relations, and power.

Facing the dragons helps you to let go of limiting patterns. Unless you let go, your system cannot grow. In the next chapter, you will look at the Dissolution Cycle and methods for facilitating karmic change—changing the cause and effect in transformation.

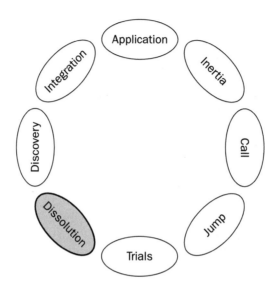

What must be let go for the new to emerge?

7

Dissolution and Compassion

ARTHUR JAY HAS A PICTURE OF HIMSELF standing on the Great Wall of China. He often jokes that the first thought he had on that occasion was a voice from childhood: "Finish your food; think of all those starving children in China." That picture has special meaning to AJ because soon after it was taken, he was offered a job at TCom. He had dreamed of building his own international organization, a place of high adventure for like-minded explorers of frontiers. He soon learned that many walls stood between his dream and the frontiers of organization building.

In Chapter Two, you learned about the intertwining journeys of AJ and his organization. The journey maps of AJ and his group show that, in order to truly transform and to create room for the new to emerge, they must take down the walls erected by the limiting organization patterns and perspectives. Specifically, they have to let go of the wounds of unresolved conflicts, dependence on functional expertise, and the exclusivity of an elite core. This letting go and adopting new creative patterns is the challenge of the Dissolution Cycle.

Dissolution can be a turning point to a higher state of development. As a seed dies so that a flower can grow, so letting go can lead to new blossoming. In mythology, dissolution and rebirth is a universal theme, for example, the Phoenix rising from ashes or the emergence of a new world after flood and fire (Campbell, 1990). Physicist Fritjof Capra's (1982) *The Turning Point* elaborates the rising of new culture out of the crisis and decay of old ideas. In this chapter, we will focus more closely on the actual process of achieving expanded awareness and functioning. I call this process karmic change. Karma refers to cause and effect (Chopra, 1994); thus, karmic change is about influencing the dissolution process so as to produce a more creative adaptation to change. I will present two ways of facilitating karmic change—the Karmic Change Method and Scripts in Our Heads (Allen, 1991)—and their applications in organizations. These two methods are in part inspired by work on the mind's transformative power, first popularized by French psychotherapist Émile Coué (1857–1926), and later found in works by authors such as Robert Collier (1926), Donald Wilson (1979), Shad Helmstetter (1987), and Ernest Holmes (1988). You will look at how compassion can be a catalyst for expanded awareness and functioning (Osbon, 1991). Compassion is the heart energy of lotus 4 in the Lotus Path. Lotus 4 bridges the lower lotuses (1, 2, 3) and upper lotuses (5, 6, 7). You have looked at the three lower lotuses in Chapter Six. You will look at the upper lotuses in Chapter Eight. This chapter is focused on Lotus 4. Let's begin by learning more about dissolution and the role of compassion in transformation.

The Meaning of Dissolution

Due to its connotation of death, dissolution is often viewed negatively. Dissolution usually means liquefying, fading, ending, or disappearing. In my Archetypal Change Journey, I refer to a state between the disappearance of the old and the emergence of the new during systems transformation. In mythologies, dissolution tales often involve death and rebirth through flood, fire, descent into the abyss, or being swallowed by a beast. In organizations, dissolution can occur as a result of physical breakup, as in restructuring or the adoption of new mindsets from cultural change. In the Archetypal Change Journey, dissolution is a point at which more creative development can occur.

As a form of chaos, dissolution can be viewed as a deviation from the traditional organization ideal of equilibrium (Marshak, 1993a). However, the new sciences now offer more liberating insights. Dissolution or turbulence is part of a system's capability to self-organize positive adaptation (Prigogine & Stengers, 1984). Through dissolution, a system can reach for a more creative version of itself. This critical juncture is referred to as the bifurcation point (Wheatley, 1994). What is bifurcation? How is it relevant to organization change?

Dissolution as Turning Point

Bifurcation literally means the forking or branching in a path. It is the turning point. In the evolution of a system, bifurcation is a vital instant in which the iterative feedback of something as delicate as, say, the flap of a butterfly's wings from a great distance, builds sufficient energy to propel the system in a new direction. Through amplification of iterative feedback, the bifurcation point can offer multiple possibilities. It can be viewed as a zone of freedom of choice. The system is offered multiple possible futures for itself. Sometimes, the available choices are so numerous and momentous that it can be a time of chaos. Bifurcation points are a summary of the change paths in a system's evolution. For example, the human embryo's journey through stages where it resembles a fish, then an amphibian, and then a reptile is a historical record of bifurcation points (Briggs & Peat, 1990). Dissolution of old forms is necessary to promote bifurcation opportunities. In the Archetypal Change Journey, change agents can positively influence a system's adaptation at bifurcation junctures through the art of compassion (Sambhava, 1994). How can compassion influence adaptation?

Compassion and Transformation

In human terms, dissolution can bring suffering. The antidote to suffering is compassion. Compassion can trigger a leap to expanded consciousness or a higher-level development (Osbon, 1991). How can compassion do that? I never understood this puzzle until I looked back at my own cancer journey. I was not able to heal and move on until I discovered compassion in my own heart and applied it to my suffering self. I realized that no amount of intellectual reasoning can master death. I accepted death as a condition for life. That moment of despair and compassion was a bifurcation point to recovery (Allen, 1995). Let me explore further how compassion can lead to higher awareness or enlightenment.

Compassion is made up of the root words "com" meaning together and "pati" to suffer. So it implies feeling pity or sorrow for the suffering or trouble of others, accompanied by the urge to help. It means opening our hearts to include others in our love. Compassion is the energy of Lotus 4, the heart energy center of the Lotus

Path introduced in Chapter Six. In Sufism, compassion is himma, the power of the heart (Platt, 1999). The act of compassion dissolves the egocentric boundary that rigidly separates the self from others. Such an act recognizes that, at the universal energy level, we are all one (Campbell & Moyers, 1991). The art of compassion is the capacity to offer kind and informed help to guide a system toward positive evolution. Practically, this means helping a system to let go of limiting fears and stereotypes and to adopt liberating visions and ideas. Two methods to do that will be discussed later.

Compassion is a key to enlightenment and transcendence in a system's evolution. Compassion is the central message of the Grail Quest (Campbell & Moyers, 1991). You may believe that enlightenment and transcendence are too esoteric for business organizations. I invite you to think of these two concepts as expanding awareness and creative adaptations. Enlightenment is the realization of a larger realm of existence. The act of enlightenment dissolves the limiting boundary of perception and intellectual or head knowledge. Enlightenment is awareness overcoming ignorance. Ignorance is the root of fears and suffering (Sambhava, 1994). Because a system's awareness is always imperfect, ignorance and suffering are part of its existence. The antidote to suffering from ignorance is to accept the limits of intellectual knowledge and to be open to spiritual inspirations. The discovery of spiritual inspirations or epiphanies takes a system to a higher level of awareness and functioning.

Transcendence is the capacity to rise above ignorance and live in enlightenment or expanding awareness. A transcendent system is one that is able to evolve from limiting self-organization to creative adaptation. By practicing compassion, change agents can facilitate a system's enlightenment and transcendence. The wisdom traditions of the world teach us that enlightenment and transcendence are effective strategies for thriving in turbulent environments (Cooper, 1992). In Chapter Eight, we will look at using spiritual or high-quality energies to effect change. Now, let's look at some compassion practices.

Practicing Compassion

Confronting limiting ideas can trigger guilt, shame, and self-hatred. The following practices can offer support for this suffering. In the Tibetan tradition, dying, like birth, is a communal affair. The wisdom and compassion of the lama/priest are critical. A key role of the lama is to *suffer with* the dying person through empathetic presence. Enlightening instruction at dissolution or death can dissolve ignorance and fears (Sambhava, 1994). When organizations have to let go of old patterns, change practitioners can help through their empathetic presence. Empathetic presence includes making oneself available, offering responsive listening, attending to people and situations with loving kindness, and providing constructive feedback.

In dissolution, people and systems can fall apart. Timely information and compassionate instruction before and during dissolution can facilitate creative adaptation. In the Tibetan tradition, the lama helps people prepare for dissolution and reincarnation by encouraging critical insights, positive emotional habits, and right actions. During the period of dying, the lama offers prayers and instruction to the living and the dying. Change agents can gain insights from the lama's role.

The Lama's Role: Insights for Change Agents

- Before dissolution, help people acquire the appropriate perspectives, awareness, and skills related to creative adaptation.

- Prepare people for what they can expect during dissolution.

- Create and offer customized scripts to guide and support creative adaptations.

- Offer empathetic presence.

- Open your heart to countenance suffering.

As change agents, you can provide wise guidance throughout a system's dissolution. In pre-dissolution, you can increase awareness of how thoughts affect actions and outcomes. During dissolution, you can provide step-by-step guidance in choosing a desired future. In the next section, we will look at two methods for influencing dissolution in this way and facilitating karmic change.

Facilitating Karmic Change

Karma refers to cause and effect of a pattern (Chopra, 1994). I use karma in a non-religious sense. Thoughts, feelings, and actions are karmic in that they engender consequences of further thoughts, feelings, and actions. Effective thoughts, feelings, and actions lead to effective outcomes (Collier, 1926; Helmstetter, 1987). They can bias the adaptive process toward a desired future. The karma of effective action in biological evolution has been explored by Humberto Maturana and Francisco

Varela in *The Tree of Knowledge* (1992). By understanding how karma operates, a system can shape its own change. When a system is unaware of the content of its operating system, it is doomed to reproduce the same results mindlessly. To break the pattern, you can use what I describe as the Karmic Change Method.

Karmic Change Method

The Karmic Change Method (KCM) can increase awareness of the subtle changes in the cause-and-effect relationship in transformation. The Karmic Change Method, illustrated in Figure 7.1, is a circular loop showing the interconnectedness between systemic programming and outcome.

Figure 7.1. The Karmic Change Method

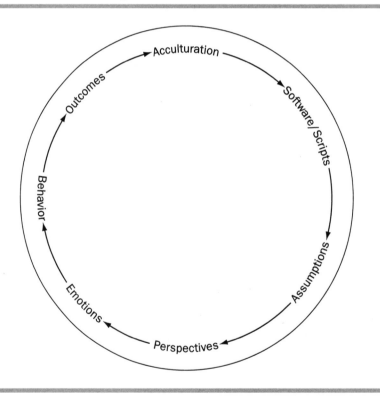

The KCM loop is made up of the karmic programs, karmic assumptions, karmic perspectives, karmic emotions, karmic behavior, and karmic outcomes. These components run in a continuous feedback loop to create the results in the karmic program. This is how KCM works: Through *acculturation,* a system develops operational *software* for self-organization. The software is made up of knowledge, memories, experience, and *scripts* that sustain the life of a system. The software creates *assumptions* about reality. The assumptions then shape *perspectives* toward people, events, and situations. Perspectives influence feelings and *emotions* about people, events, and situations. A system can feel good, bad, excited, fearful, or dejected or experience other fears and desires. Emotions influence *behavior.* Behavior creates *outcomes.* Outcomes reinforce the system's operational software, and so on. The loop cycles iteratively to sustain the karmic effect.

In the KCM loop, ideas in the operational system are continually becoming reality. Once an idea is installed in a system's operational program, the whole system will work together to maintain the assumptions, perspectives, emotions, and behavior associated with the idea. For example, if part of my programming includes stereotypes about persons of culture X background being unreliable, the outcome of my working relationship with someone from that background may be negatively affected. Instead of evaluating my own karmic process, I may find it easier to blame the X person and confirm my stereotype. The effect of programming can be long-lasting—recall Arthur Jay's childhood memory flashback on the Great Wall of China.

If a system is unaware of its own karmic process, then the karmic loop can continue to produce the same results. Karmic awareness can change the results. In a loop, you can intervene at any point: software, emotions, or actions. Choose an approach that is comfortable for you. KCM works in conjunction with Scripts in Our Heads, which will be described later in this chapter. KCM is a simple exercise. The following guidelines show you how to use it with a group.

Step 1. Start with a personal approach. Ask participants to identify do's and don'ts from their childhood and how these affect perspectives, feelings, behavior, and outcomes in their lives. Using the karmic loop in Figure 7.1, illustrate how these childhood do's and don'ts create karmic outcomes.

Step 2. Ask participants to name some do's and don'ts in their organizations. Using the karmic loop, show how these do's and don'ts affect organizational outcomes.

Step 3. Identify new do's and follow through the karmic loop to see what new results can be produced. These three steps are good introductory exercises to other applications in this chapter.

Variations: Work backward on the karmic loop by identifying an organizational result and ask what behavior, emotions, perspectives, and scripts in the karmic loop produce that result. Work from the middle of the loop—identify a corporate behavior and go clockwise or counter-clockwise through the whole karmic loop.

Tips for Using the Karmic Change Method

- Facilitate with respect and confidence.

- Trust the process.

- Do some team building prior to this activity.

- Explain the rationale and process clearly.

- Adapt the sequence to match change approaches. For example, behavior may come before perspectives, and so on.

▶ Application: Do's and Don'ts in TCom

The risk management unit in TCom wanted to address confusion over decision making. Daryn and Julee helped the unit use the three steps of the KCM.

Step 1. The group identified childhood do's and don'ts. Here are some of their examples: "Don't talk back to your elders" (relationship to authority); "Wear clean underwear in case you are run over by a truck" (honor, shame); "Don't tell lies" (honesty); "Finish your food" (thrift); and "Wash behind your ears" (cleanliness). The group then explored the values and mores (shown in parentheses) that were being transmitted by the do's and don'ts and how these created karmic effect in their adult perspectives, feelings, and behavior. For example, one participant said that, as a result of "Don't talk back to your elders," he was often reluctant to contradict authority figures such as managers.

Step 2. The group identified organization do's and don'ts. For example, in TCom, a "do" was "bring solutions, not problems." Some outcomes of this were (1) that people didn't explore problems with their managers and (2) that people offered solutions before understanding the problem. These outcomes had a negative impact on the unit's performance.

Step 3. The group brainstormed do's and don'ts that were more helpful to their current situation. For example, the group decided a helpful "do" was "Take risks and use your judgment." The desired outcome from this "do" was people holding themselves accountable for assessing each situation and deciding on appropriate action. ◄

In the above example, you see how simple steps can begin to disturb a karmic loop and create change. In the next application, we'll look at two other ways of using the KCM.

► Application: Changing Outcomes

The Technical Services (TS) Division was falling apart. The group was under siege by work overload. Half of its staff felt burned out. A tenth of the staff was already on stress leave. There had been uncertainty about the top leadership position for seven months, and there was talk the division might be outsourced. A key client group revolted and refused to have further contact with the division.

Retrospective Karma

In the retrospective karma, the group went through the KCM loop (Figure 7.1) in a counter-clockwise fashion, starting by identifying current outcomes and moving backward to identify the karmic assumptions that produced the current outcomes. Following is a summary of the TS Division's process:

Karmic Outcome. Participants identified current outcomes: unbearable workload; too much overtime; work/home imbalance; lack of champion at executive level.

Karmic Behavior. They identified behaviors that contributed to current outcome: Avoiding contact with the world outside; keeping their noses to the grindstone; socializing only within the group; working incredible hours; not communicating upward with management or outward with client groups.

Karmic Emotions. They identified emotions that may have shaped behavior: Feeling victimized; too stressed out; can't afford to lose time; fearful of playing politics; feeling like second-class citizens. Statements reveal they also suspect knowledge and skills are not up-to-date due to lack of time for training and development.

Karmic Perspectives. They identified perspectives that color emotions. Statements included the following: It is us against the whole world; we are not worthy; I have no energy to focus on anything else except work.

Karmic Assumptions. They identified underlying assumptions that may have given rise to these perspectives: Work hard and you will be rewarded; our division is just adding to the overhead costs in this organization; we are not producers of value.

Prospective Karma

Having identified what produced the group's current outcome through retrospective karma, the participants looked forward to a new karma. They started by identifying the desired new karmic outcome and worked backward to the new karmic assumptions needed to produce the desired outcome. Here are the steps they took.

New Karmic Outcome. They identified desired outcomes: Increased staffing; a leader respected by the larger organization; having their contributions valued.

New Karmic Behavior. They identified actions that would produce the desired outcomes: Meeting with the executive committee to explore solutions; an increase in staffing; dialogue sessions with the "revolting" client; regular open house and roundtable meetings with client systems; the designing of customer-oriented processes; developing and implementing a client relations campaign to present a distinct identity and educate clients on the division's vision, mission, and goals; creating a profile of each staff member to replace the division's nameless image; assigning representatives to each client system.

New Karmic Emotions. They identified feelings that would engender the desired behavior: Adopting and projecting positive feelings about the worth of the division; feeling excited about being part of a growing enterprise; viewing the larger organization as creative, empathetic.

New Karmic Perspectives. They identified perspectives that would produce positive emotions: Adopting an assertive attitude; holding a balanced perspective; responding to requests with confidence.

New Karmic Assumptions. They identified assumptions that could shape positive perspectives: TS Division works in partnership with its clients; the division is strategic to the overall organization's wealth and well-being; everyone in the division is a champion and a change agent who can take positive action to produce desired outcomes.

Using the prospective karma, the division created an action plan and subsequently implemented many of the actions. The division was successful in acquiring the needed staffing as well as a new leader who was well-respected in the organization. The TS Division used the worksheet in Exhibit 7.1 in creating karmic change. ◄

Exhibit 7.1. Karmic Change Worksheet

Instructions: Complete the following ten steps.

1. **Karmic Outcome.** Identify a current outcome in your organization that you want to change:

2. **Karmic Behavior.** Identify behaviors that contribute to the current outcome:

Exhibit 7.1. Karmic Change Worksheet, Cont'd

3. **Karmic Emotions.** Identify emotions that may have shaped the identified behaviors:

4. **Karmic Perspectives.** Identify perspectives that may have influenced the identified emotions:

5. **Karmic Assumptions.** Identify the underlying assumptions that may have given rise to the identified perspectives:

6. **New Karmic Outcome.** Identify a desired outcome:

7. **New Karmic Behaviors.** Identify new behaviors that will produce the desired outcome:

Exhibit 7.1. Karmic Change Worksheet, Cont'd

8. **New Karmic Emotions.** Identify the emotions that will engender the desired behaviors:

9. **New Karmic Perspectives.** Identify the perspectives that will produce the desired emotions:

10. **New Karmic Assumptions.** Identify the assumptions that can shape the desired perspectives:

The Karmic Change Method shows you how the karmic loop works. Now we will take a more detailed look at the techniques for changing the content of karmic programs.

Scripts in Our Heads

Karmic patterns usually develop through cultural conditioning. To bias the adaptation in a desired direction, you rewrite the scripts that direct karma. I call the method for doing that Scripts in Our Heads. The key purpose is to replace mental scripts that produce undesirable outcomes. You can use this method with individuals or in a group. If you are working with more than eight people, it is best to divide the group into smaller subgroups of four to five participants. There are four key steps in Scripts in Our Heads.

Step 1. Review. To review is to look again at what has been there all along. This step is best done in a low-key mode. Encourage a relaxed mood among the people you are working with. Then identify the change topic. This could be a system, a situation, or an issue within the organization. Focus your mind on the identified change topic. Keeping an open mind, and retiring censoring or judgmental inclinations, let ideas, feelings, and awareness related to the change topic float naturally to the surface.

Crystallize the thoughts or feelings into statements. Write these down on paper or a computer screen, one statement at a time. As you write out the statements, leave a space between them and number them. Reviewing is essentially a brainstorming process. Try to crystallize the thoughts/feelings/awareness as descriptively as possible. There are no right or wrong answers. Honesty is important. Stop the review when you have eight to twelve sentences about the topic. If you've been working with subgroups, reconvene the entire group. Ask members from each subgroup to read the statements to the whole group. Have the whole group debrief their reactions to the review statements. Identify the feelings. Depending on the topic, the group may feel anger, shame, guilt, hilarity, or embarrassment.

Step 2. Reverse, Reaffirm, or Create. Consider each of the statements that surfaced during the review. If a statement is negative, reverse it and make it into a positive statement. If a statement is positive, reaffirm and reinforce it. If you find that you cannot improve the review statements using the reverse or reaffirm technique, you can create a different statement to serve as a new script. For example, in Application 3 (see next section), one of TCom's review statements is "There is a lack of gender and ethnic diversity in TCom management." Instead of reversing or reaffirming the statement, the TCom group came up with a different statement for a new script: "TCom is sought after as a place of employment by men and women from diverse backgrounds." Do this step almost mechanically. That means disengaging the skeptical censor. This step represents a place for choice and decision— the bifurcation point in system evolution. The individual or group is choosing a different future.

In a group, debrief by asking different participants to present the reversed, reaffirmed, or new statements. Offer an opportunity for all participants to talk about their reactions. Explore why this process was difficult. Identify the feelings. Skepticism, embarrassment, self-consciousness, and a sense of frivolity are common.

Step 3. Reinforce. The goal is to have the reversed or reaffirmed statements as the new instructions in the operating software. Due to karmic momentum, the rejection rate of new scripts can be very high. Gradually the old scripts will reassert their karmic power. The old scripts have built powerful colonies within the system. They have put down roots in the form of emotional attachments and fears. Show Figure 7.2 to illustrate the tenacity of old programming.

Figure 7.2. Anatomy of a Stereotype

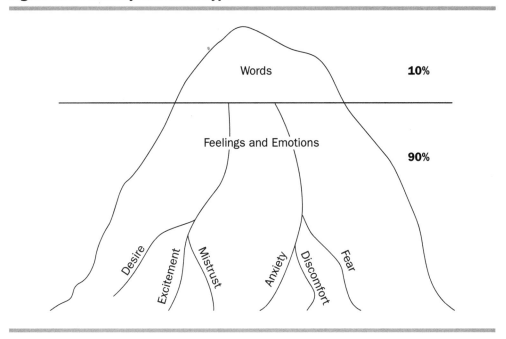

A stereotype is a prejudgment that is absorbed into a program or system. It stays and roots itself there. The force of the actual words used accounts for, say, 10 percent of the power of a stereotype. But 90 percent of the power lies in its emotional roots, deep in the system (Wilson, 1979). These roots are nurtured by societal influence and conditioning. To successfully plant the new scripts and ensure successful reprogramming, you have to use similar nurturing. For this, you need to mobilize the nonlinear, intuitive brain.

Here are the steps for installing a new script: Take each reversed statement and create an image, scenario, or visualization of that statement. The scenario should include the five senses: sight, sound, smell, touch, and taste. Exaggerate the scenario. Make the visualization cartoon-like to enhance the rooting. You can have fun with this process. Be as creative as you want. Repeat this process until you have a series of virtual desired realities.

Step 4. Routinize. The last step is routine reinforcement. Integrate the affirmations and scenarios into daily routines. Bring up scenarios in your mind or on computer screens. Use the affirmations and scenarios to guide policies, procedures, and practices. The key is to become aware of these four steps and to be able to use them as a matter of routine. By taking these small actions, you can create new karmic reality.

Tips for Using Scripts in Our Heads

- Scripts in Our Heads is a useful method for cultural and behavioral change.

- Use this method in conjunction with the Karmic Change Method and Anatomy of a Stereotype.

- Customize to audience needs.

- Test the process for yourself first.

- Do not create positive group stereotypes in place of negative group stereotypes. Stereotyping limits creativity.

Now let's look at some applications of Scripts in Our Heads.

▶ Application: Fostering a Diversity Culture

TCom used Scripts in Our Heads to create a more positive environment for diversity. You will recall from previous chapters that Julee was assigned the responsibility for the Diversity Survey at TCom and Linco. Her boss, Arthur Jay (AJ), wanted to take the process further to create an environment welcoming to diversity. Julee, with the help of Daryn, Arente, and Hingram, facilitated sessions with a cross-section of TCom employees. They used the KCM and Scripts in Our Heads to frame and focus the sessions. Their use of the KCM was similar to the process described in Application 1, "Do's and Don'ts in TCom."

After presenting the KCM framework and leading the group through the KCM exercise, the facilitators helped participants select their change topic—in this case TCom's diversity culture. Then participants proceeded with the four steps.

Step 1. Review. Working in small groups in a low-key and relaxed manner, participants focused on the change topic and surfaced scripts in their heads. Here is a sample of their scripts:

- Diversity is not viewed as an important issue in TCom.
- There is a lack of gender and ethnic diversity in TCom management.
- The diversity within TCom's current management team is not tapped.
- There is an "us" and "them" mentality between expatriates and national employees in offshore locations.
- Ideas are valued according to the rank of the contributors.
- People don't speak up in meetings for fear of being humiliated.
- TCom has good leaders.
- TCom has dedicated employees.

The facilitators invited the small groups to read out their scripts and talk about their experiences.

Step 2. Reverse, Reaffirm, or Create. For each statement from Step 1, participants reversed the negative ones, reaffirmed the positives, or wrote new scripts. The sample new statements are listed below. (The parenthetical remarks following each item indicate whether it is a reversal, a reaffirmation, or a new creation.)

- Diversity is the secret of TCom's global success. (reverse)
- TCom management is a dynamic and diverse group of world-class executives. (reverse)
- TCom is sought after as a place of employment by men and women from diverse backgrounds. (create)

- TCom management is setting a good example by learning and applying the skills of synergy and partnership within the group. (reverse)

- TCom is developing a new global business model in which collaboration and co-creation among different employees are critical values and practices. (reverse)

- Ideas are valued according to their quality. TCom is a successful global enterprise powered by ideas. (reverse)

- TCom meetings are summits of champions. TCom employees enjoy speaking up freely. (reverse)

- TCom has great leaders. (reaffirm)

- TCom has dedicated world-class employees. (reaffirm)

At first, participants found it difficult to envision positive statements. After a while they got on with the activity. After Step 2, participants talked about their experience.

Step 3: Reinforce. Referring back to the KCM loop (Figure 7.1), and showing Anatomy of a Stereotype (Figure 7.2), the facilitators explained how to do Step 3—reinforce the new scripts by using their creative imaginations. The facilitators assigned two statements to each small group and asked each group to come up with a creative imaginative scenario for each statement. Here is a sampling of scenarios generated by participants for the nine new scripts created in Step 2.

- TCom is featured in a leading business magazine for its success in creating a diversity advantage.

- A picture of a long line of women and men from diverse backgrounds clamoring to join TCom management.

- A dramatic skit in which TCom management announces that, as a result of its success with creating synergy, it is establishing a profit center to provide synergy consulting services.

- A series of creative visualizations: TCom employees, including expats and local nationals, are enthusiastically collaborating with one another in various meetings and projects.

- A creative design of a logo: "TCom: Success powered by ideas."
- A computer-generated graphic of beaming TCom employees in meetings, with a profusion of light bulbs over their heads.
- An ode to TCom leaders.
- A drawing of a diverse TCom workforce plastered with medals and awards.

Facilitators invited the small groups to share their creative products from Step 3. Participants talked about their experience and commented on the quality of the energy in the different steps.

Step 4. Routinize. Facilitators invited the participants to come up with simple ways to help routinize the new scripts. Posting new scripts and graphics on the web, removing barriers in recruitment and other employment practices, using the new scripts in their thinking and planning, and incorporating diversity as a competency in the performance appraisal system were some ideas taken up. ◀

Scripts in Our Heads showed TCom how to create new scripts to inspire change in its diversity culture. In the next application, we'll look at how an individual can use Scripts in Our Heads to deal with a career crisis.

▶ Application: Step Back from Oblivion

Gilda, an experienced manager competent in several disciplines, was thrilled to be assigned to head up regional operations. She worked almost night and day to meet the demands of a growing global operation. But it was soon apparent that she was sinking in an executive council that valued charisma and aggressiveness. Gilda's low-key style was neither understood nor appreciated. She struggled to be heard and seen. After months of debilitating uncertainty about her position, she was replaced. Gilda sought coaching from Arente.

Gilda was at a bifurcation point. The dissolution of her position could open new opportunities or it could be the end of a highly promising career. Gilda used the four steps of Scripts in Our Heads to steer the dissolution into a positive career reincarnation. The following is a summary of Gilda's four steps.

Step 1. Review. Focusing on her life, Gilda identified that what was most critical to her were career success and good personal relationships with her family. The two were interrelated. Taking one area at a time, Gilda focused and let issues surface. She crystallized the vague thoughts and feelings into clear statements. Following are some of Gilda's review statements:

- I am stressed and anxious about my career and personal relationships.
- My stress is affecting my health.
- I don't have what it takes to be a good leader.
- My voice is not heard in the executive council.
- My staff do appreciate me.
- The executive council is an old boys' club.

Step 2. Reverse, Reaffirm, Create. Gilda reversed the negative statements, strengthened the positive ones, and, in some instances, created new scripts, resulting in the following statements.

- I am clear about what I want for my career and personal relationships and I am getting great satisfaction from both. (reverse and create)
- I take good care of my health by incorporating my favorite pastimes into my routines. (reverse and create)
- I am a good leader and I have what it takes to excel. (reverse)
- My voice is heard. I express my convictions clearly, calmly, and firmly. (reverse and create)
- My staff appreciate my talents and contribution. (reaffirm)
- I work in an open and congenial work environment where my talents are well used. (create)

Step 3. Reinforce. Gilda created a series of positive and imaginative visualizations of the positive statements. She made two sets of positive scripts. Set 1 used "I" statements: "I am a good leader." "My voice is heard." "I express my convictions clearly, calmly and firmly." Set 2 used "You" statements: "Gilda, you are a good leader with very special talents." "You are bold and creative." "You state your visions and views with conviction and clarity."

Step 4. Routinize. Gilda practiced reading her new scripts out loud. Gilda also used videotaping to increase awareness of her body language. She practiced the axis mundi stance—physically standing firm on her immovable axis, that is, standing her ground, claiming the ground she stands on with conviction. She also practiced projecting her voice with the intention of being heard. Gilda enlisted her family's help in listening to her read the scripts.

As an incentive, Gilda rewarded herself by choosing to do something she enjoyed daily (swimming) and monthly (sailing). Three months into the program, Gilda was given a new assignment she felt suited her talents. Gilda used the worksheets in Exhibits 7.1 and 7.2 to help her practice the four steps of Scripts in Our Heads. ◀

The two worksheets are variations of the four steps. Use either for your own purposes.

Exhibit 7.2. Scripts in Our Heads Worksheet I

Instructions: Identify your change topic and complete all four steps.

The change topic is _____

Step 1. Review. Focusing on the change topic, crystallize your thoughts, feelings, or concerns into statements and write these down, one statement at a time.

Exhibit 7.2. Scripts in Our Heads Worksheet I, Cont'd

Step 2. Reverse, reaffirm, or create. Consider each review statement. Reverse negative review statements, reaffirm positive review statements, or create different statements to serve as new scripts.

Step 3. Reinforce. For each transformed statement from Step 2, create a sensory-rich image, scenario, or visualization.

Step 4. Routinize. Create a routine of reading the transformed statements from Step 2 and bringing to mind the sensory-rich image, scenario, or visualization from Step 3.

Exhibit 7.3. Scripts in Our Heads Worksheet II

Instructions: Identify your change topic. Come up with eight review statements. For each review statement, complete Steps 2 through 4 of Scripts in Our Heads.

Change Topic: _____

Review Statement 1:

Reverse/Reaffirm/Create:

Reinforce:

Routinize:

Review Statement 2:

Reverse/Reaffirm/Create:

Reinforce:

Routinize:

Review Statement 3:

Reverse/Reaffirm/Create:

Reinforce:

Routinize:

Review Statement 4:

Reverse/Reaffirm/Create:

Reinforce:

Routinize:

Exhibit 7.3. Scripts in Our Heads Worksheet II, Cont'd

Review Statement 5:

Reverse/Reaffirm/Create:

Reinforce:

Routinize:

Review Statement 6:

Reverse/Reaffirm/Create:

Reinforce:

Routinize:

Review Statement 7:

Reverse/Reaffirm/Create:

Reinforce:

Routinize:

Review Statement 8:

Reverse/Reaffirm/Create:

Reinforce:

Routinize:

I have used these tools with a wide range of organizations and audiences. Individuals and groups respond to them because they make intuitive sense. They are effective coaching tools. The key is for change agents to develop personal comfort with them before using them with others. The following practice activities can increase your comfort level with these tools.

Practice Activities

1. Identify a dominating pattern in your organization. Using the Karmic Change Method, explain how this pattern is created. How would you apply the Karmic Change Method to change this dominating pattern?

2. In your own practice, what pattern must be let go? Use the four steps of Scripts in Our Heads to create a desired new pattern.

Summary and Preview

Due to cultural conditioning, human systems often suffer in dissolution. This chapter described the Dissolution Cycle as the place where old patterns end and more creative ones emerge. I explained the importance of compassion in opening you to the higher awareness and functioning of enlightenment and transcendence. I presented the Karmic Change Method and Scripts in Our Heads for replacing limiting ideas with creative ones. Dissolution prepares a system to discover the gifts of expanded awareness and functioning.

In the next chapter, you will look at the Discovery Cycle and learn a method called Three Turns of Transformation. This method can help you access the higher energies of radiance, rapture, and bliss.

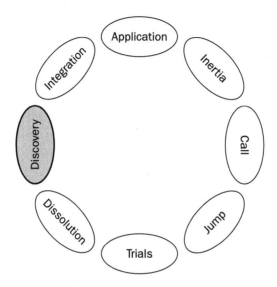

What gifts of change are in the offing?

(8)

Discovery and Epiphany

ON THE 21ST CENTURY, BUSINESS IS conducted at the speed of fiberoptic channeled light. To thrive, organizations want to learn the secrets of fast and meaningful transformation. As change agents, how do you help? In this chapter, we will return to the seven energies of the Lotus Path to tap into more transformation secrets. In the Dissolution Cycle, you learned that the practice of compassion can facilitate a leap to expanded awareness and functioning. This chapter will show you the experiences and methods for achieving expanded awareness and functioning. You will learn how practitioner Daryn uses these methods to enhance her practice. You will read about three transformative epiphanies, flashes of revelation that expand awareness and functioning. Many scientific discoveries are made in flashes of intuitive insight or moments of synchronicity (von Franz, 1969). Archimedes' shout of "Eureka!" and Isaac Newton's falling-apple inspiration are just two examples of transformative epiphanies. Physicist David Peat (1991), building on Jung's ideas of archetype and synchronicity, proposed that synchronicities or epiphanies are organizing patterns and experiences of the universe.

Synchronicity/epiphany bridges matter and mind and transcends the limits of rational science. Peat sees the investigation of synchronicity/epiphany as key to the new science of wholeness.

In this book, I view epiphanies as insightful and intuitive experiences that can expand the boundaries of existing awareness and functioning. In the wisdom tradition, epiphanies bring enlightenment and transcendence (Anonymous South Asian Sages, 1999). Epiphanies can be regarded as high-grade and high-speed energies in human systems. That is, epiphanies can help you accomplish change in a fast and seemingly effortless manner. Epiphanies enable people and organizations to rise above limiting patterns to discover new sources of creativity. In short, epiphanies are the gifts of discovery. Let's now explore the Discovery Cycle and practices that facilitate epiphanies.

The Gifts of Discovery

Discovery refers to an unexpected find or sudden recognition in the course of a search. The Discovery Cycle is the high point in the transformation journey. In mythological tales, discovery is a time of creation and rebirth. It is the point at which the heroes and heroines have wrestled with the obstructing dragon and snatch the pearl from its mouth. Or they are finally led to the treasure cave or see the Promised Land. The dragon's pearl, treasure cave, the Promised Land, and other mythological tropes such as the tree of life, magic flute, and the meeting with gods and goddesses, are all metaphors for the discovery of authentic power. Discovery gives you newfound energy to achieve your true purpose and potential. Following are some qualities of the Discovery Cycle.

Clarity and light now infuse the system, displacing ambiguity and shadow. An organization or person can perceive what was previously hidden from them. The taken-for-granted now assumes an aura of radiance and desirability. In discovery, a system is enlightened.

The discovery experience makes possible new visions, goals, and values that were once inconceivable. A new structure, a new culture, a new business, a new market is now realizable. The system is given new revelations about itself. The quest of the Archetypal Change Journey is almost accomplished. You are face to face now with the unimagined or the unexpected. The system is changed. In discovery, you and your organization are invited to use energies in new ways and be open to epiphanies.

Epiphany is an intense experience of revelation, a sudden, exquisite insight. Divisive boundaries melt away. Conventional meanings dissolve. There is a feeling of being at one with all that is. People and organizations that are touched by epiphanies are irrevocably transformed.

The three great manifestations of epiphanies are *radiance, rapture,* and *bliss.* Radiance is the experience of illuminating light. Rapture is the experience of joyful identification with the creative energy in all beings. Bliss is the wondrous experience of unity and timelessness. These experiences dissolve boundaries kept in place by limiting fears or desires and enable a system to develop the confidence and competence to adopt a new way of being.

This leads to further discussion of the seven energies of the Lotus Path first introduced in Chapter Six. You will look at the energies of Lotus 5, 6, and 7 and learn the awakened and unawakened experiences associated with each. Later, you will look at practical applications of these three remaining Lotus energies. Incidentally, if the word lotus bothers you, substitute energy.

Lotus 5: Radiance Energy

Lotus 5 is about light. The focus is shining an inner light to reveal the demons within. This is the center of spiritual work. The demons within are the fears, desires, and all the social-biological programming that is imprinted in a system's operating software. The awakened radiance energy helps you disengage your censor and face the internal demons with courage and equanimity. The energy teaches you to be kind and forgiving. Once you release energies trapped by fears and desires, you can be free to experience luminosity, an experience of great intimacy with the self and with the world, as if suddenly the world and you have become one radiant light. What was hidden is now revealed. What was opaque is now transparent.

Feeling grounded is a vital aspect of Lotus 5. You are grounded in being and connection with the creative energy. You develop the capacity to countenance greed, pride, selfishness, and envy with courage and realism. Connectedness is also important. You discover your capacity for experiential knowing or knowing through the heart. Such knowing connects you with universal truth.

When Lotus 5 is unawakened, you may experience projections. That is, you focus on the pride, envy, greed, cowardice, malice, and similar "demons" in others. By not recognizing these demons within, you become haunted by them everywhere else. That can lead to persecution. You can become preoccupied with discarding people you perceive as weak, imperfect, or dissimilar.

Lotus 6: Rapture Energy

Lotus 6 is the energy center of joy, love, and ecstasy. Life becomes a rapture, a song. You see divinity in all things and recognize the sacred in the mundane. You feel partnership with all beings. When Lotus 6 is awakened, you experience grace, the feeling of divine ease and abundance. A system in grace accomplishes its visions and goals effortlessly. Problems resolve themselves as if by divine intervention. You can rejoice in wonder; you savor the capacity to marvel at the diversity and magnificent creativity of the universe. The world is a parade of songs, shapes, and shades. It sparkles with visions and delight. You are filled with zest and the capacity to live gloriously. Through zest, a system can sustain continuous creativity.

When Lotus 6 is closed, you experience isolation. Although you are alive in the midst of multitudes, you feel disconnected from the flow of life. You are unable to share sorrows and joys. You may grow despondent and feel overwhelmed by your own insignificance. You see the world as an indifferent place and people as uncaring. You are torn by a sense of fragmentation. The richness and diversity of the world bring no delight. Instead, they bring confusion, uncertainty, and threat.

Lotus 7: Bliss Energy

Lotus 7 is the center of bliss. Bliss is the experience of unity and wholeness. When this energy is activated, you transcend the limiting concerns of daily survival to experience the pure joy of being alive in the here and now.

When Lotus 7 is awakened, you experience transcendence. Transcendence is freedom from divisiveness and ignorance. Boundaries dissolve. Wonder, awe, and serenity pervade. Bliss brings wholeness—the experience of one life, one light. A sense of completion and perfection prevails. Everything is as it should be. Through bliss, you are in touch with the mystery of existence. You experience the ineffable and you revel in the unknown and the unknowable.

When Lotus 7 is not open, you experience a desire to control. The unknown becomes terrifying. You try to exert control over people, events, and things. You feel a strong need for order, structure, regulation, rules, and laws. Protectionism becomes a goal. Instead of embracing the unknown as life's great experience, you try to protect yourself from the unknown by continually seeking data and rational explanation. In your eagerness to achieve rational understanding, you shut out experience and the joy of being.

You can also suffer from the dread of being alive. Life is messy and uncontrollable. The alternative to life is also not palatable. You suffer the fear of non-being.

Although alive, you are constantly preoccupied with attacks, takeover, and death.

You have now worked through each of the seven energies of the Lotus Path. The aim is to use these energies creatively to achieve high-level goals. Later in the chapter, we will look at some practical applications.

The capacity for radiance, rapture, and bliss is inherent in you and all human systems. I call this capacity the art of epiphany. By practicing this art, a human system can wisely and effortlessly make real its full potential.

The Art of Epiphany

The art of epiphany refers to the use of insightful experiences and high-grade energies in achieving transformation. This art helps you to recognize and claim the gifts of discovery—radiance, rapture, and bliss. These experiences are powerful motivators, as effective as material rewards. Epiphanies can be similar to Abraham Maslow's (1973) peak experiences. Tapping into the transformative power of peak experiences is integral to Appreciative Inquiry (Watkins & Mohr, 2001).

The art of epiphany consists of three principal practices—the Three Turns of Transformation, described below. Later, we will discuss how to use the Three Turns of Transformation in practical situations. Again, my description is in part inspired by the work of Joseph Campbell (1986, 1989).

The first practice is *to turn the illuminating light inward to experience radiance,* the energy of Lotus 5. The illuminating light is fearless awareness. When you have the courage to see what you have hidden from yourself or what the organization has hidden from itself, you are creating illuminating radiance. When you direct your penetrating awareness to the inner or hidden world, you will begin to realize that most of the monsters you see in others are really shadows of your fears and desires. By directing your awareness to the inward reality, you will soon discover an abundance of untapped energies. When you devote these energies to inner conquests, you will be less preoccupied by power fears and desires such as defeat, victimhood, aggression, or malice. These power fears and desires, discussed in the description of Lotus 3 in Chapter Six, chain you and your organization to low levels of awareness and functioning. Through radiance, you will discover new creative powers.

The second practice is *to partner with the creative energy in all creation to experience rapture,* the energy of Lotus 6. Rapture is joyful recognition and identification with the creative energy in all beings. When you experience that all creation is connected by the same vitalizing energy, you can then transcend relational fears and desires based on such things as rejection, abandonment, lust, and seduction. These fears and desires of Lotus 2 are sustained by the illusion that people and organizations are rigidly separated from each other. The experience of rapture enables you and your organization to tap into the universal creative energy. Instead of relying on what you can accomplish alone, you learn to collaborate with others to create legacies that transcend individual limits.

The third practice is *to transcend divisions and experience bliss,* the energy of Lotus 7. Bliss is the experience of unity and transcendence. You are at one with the universal creative energy. When you follow your bliss, you are doing what gives you joy and life (Campbell & Moyers, 1991); you are not held back by barriers; no obstacles can divide you from what you naturally love to do. When you do what gives you bliss, you can more easily transcend survival fears and desires such as annihilation, envy, lethargy, feeding frenzy, or greed. When you follow your bliss energy, you are more likely to be in touch with your change intention and hence are better able to achieve your creative goals. The concept of following your bliss is similar to Lao Tzu's Wu Wei, effortless action or effortless achievement referred to in Chapter One.

In the above, I discussed practices that can facilitate the experience of epiphanies. Let's visit with TCom and see how people there experience epiphanies.

TCom and Epiphanies

A noticeable characteristic of TCom is the intensity of its employees. More than a few are world-class athletes. Others have interesting and absorbing pursuits outside of work. The majority joined TCom to follow their bliss. Occasionally, in private conversations, you can catch glimpses of radiance, rapture, and bliss. In meetings, employees behave quite differently though. They doggedly adhere to their hierarchical ranks and job roles. Their meetings are devoid of light and mirth. Often, people come away with sore backs, groggy eyes, wounded feelings, and private chatter in their heads. Sometimes, they approach meetings as though on a battlefield where they must aggressively push their own agenda. Sometimes, they withdraw from participation due to fear of rejection. Other times, they regard meetings as an unavoidable evil of workplace survival—you just have to grin and bear them.

To help the group tap into new, high-grade energies in themselves and in the group, HR manager Julee and practitioner Arente show them how to use epiphany practices. As a result, the group develops new perspectives on meetings. For example, instead of the battlefield scenario, they learn to see meetings as allegorical summits for champions. The participants in meetings are geniuses. Meeting them, hearing their views, and voicing one's own views is a rare privilege. They can also regard meetings from the perspective of spiritual partnerships. Life is transient and goes in a flash. One should therefore seize every meeting opportunity to have the most productive exchange possible—to meet as true minds and co-create lasting legacies. The group can also adopt a perspective that transcends superficial divisions: Colleagues are divinities in disguise. Meetings are communions of souls where participants follow their bliss.

You can see how epiphany practices enable TCom people to see everyday transactions such as meetings in a different light. This new light brings new energies; it transforms the quality of their everyday experiences. At first, TCom people find some of the epiphany perspectives preposterous or laughable. But once they get over their own and others' skepticism, they begin to appreciate the power of epiphany to transform drudgery into radiance, rapture, and bliss. They dissolve the rigid boundaries between work and the pursuit of bliss.

The practices of epiphany can help your organizations survive and thrive in stress and turbulence. First, they tap into the high-speed and high-grade energies within you and your organizations to help deliver fast responses. Second, they enlarge your learning capacity by challenging you to rise above socially conditioned fears and desires. Third, they expand workplace motivation beyond materialism and competition to include meaning and fulfillment. Last, the art of epiphany increases zest and joy in organizations and individuals. Following is a method for applying the art of epiphany in action.

The Three Turns of Transformation

The Three Turns of Transformation is a method for converting low-level energy and preoccupations into high-level energy and goals. For example, in Chapter Five, TCom's HR manager, Julee, learns that, instead of squandering all her energy on reactive firefighting, she can use it to achieve intentional change. She also finds that, by focusing on what gives her bliss, she frees up energy she was wasting on job-security concerns.

Figure 8.1 shows the change path originating in Lotus 4, the center of heart energy. The heart bridges the lower lotus energies and the higher lotus energies.

When the heart is open, the human and the universal creative energies can communicate and freely exchange. You are now ready for the Three Turns of Transformation. Refer to Figure 8.1 as you follow the explanation below.

Figure 8.1. The Three Turns of Transformation

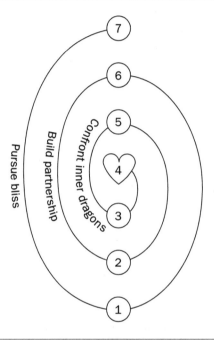

Adapted in part from *The World of Joseph Campbell: Transformation of Myth Through Time*, Joseph Campbell (1989). A production of William Free Productions, Mythology Limited, and Holoform Research Inc. Chicago, IL: Public Media Video.

The first turn is *to convert power energy into radiance.* The opening of the heart activates courage and compassion. With the energy of compassion, the transformation path descends into Lotus 3, the power center, to confront the power fears and desires. You harness the externally oriented power energy of Lotus 3 and turn it into internal light for conquering the inner demons in Lotus 5. The inward turn of enlightenment reveals that the dragons are the unacknowledged and untapped impulses within. When the light is shone inward, the system becomes radiant. This radiance brings clarity and self-awareness. Shadows and barriers are dissolved.

What was frightening and unproductive in the organization is now revealed to be useful, creative, and changeable.

The second turn is *to convert relational concerns into spiritual or creative partnerships.* The conquest of inner demons frees up previously trapped energy. From Lotus 5, take the radiant energy down to confront relational addictions attributed to Lotus 2. When relational fears and desires are dispelled, a system can rise up to Lotus 6, the center of rapture and joyful identification with diversity. Rapturous energy enables a system to form partnerships with others with trust and respect.

The third turn is *to convert consuming concerns into the pursuit of bliss.* With the partnering energy of Lotus 6, you descend and enter into the consuming fears and desires of Lotus 1. Using the rapturous energy of Lotus 6, you convert survival fears and frenzy into the pursuit of bliss in Lotus 7. The experience of bliss enables you to transcend the distracting fears and desires to live your true purpose and potential in the here and now.

The three turns show how to direct and convert volatile energies to effect transformation. You may have noticed that the Three Turns of Transformation in Figure 8.1 combine the linear arrow path (the vertical alignment of the seven energy centers) with the cyclical spiral turns. Using the three turns, you can help clients achieve fast targets (arrow value), while staying centered and purposeful even amidst turbulent change (spiral value). Next, we'll look at applications of the Three Turns of Transformation.

Daryn is a successful organization development consultant. (You have read in previous chapters about her work at Linco and TCom.) Here, you will see how Daryn uses the Three Turns of Transformation to enhance her practice.

▶ Application: Transforming the Change Agent

Daryn's key strengths are her client focus and her ability to speak the language of business. In recent years, Daryn has noticed that some of her clients have shown a keen interest in including more spiritual awareness at work. Daryn had the same interest herself but hesitated for fear of losing credibility. Daryn wanted to bring greater freedom and balance to her work. Using the Lotus Path, Daryn first assessed her current experience:

- Lotus 1—Consuming Energy: After fifteen years as an OD consultant, Daryn still had survival fears. She worried about maintaining her income every year. She found herself measuring her own worth by her yearly income.

- Lotus 2—Relational Energy: Daryn wanted more time to connect with family, friends, and colleagues. Yet she often felt guilty when away from work.

- Lotus 3—Power Energy: Daryn wanted to enhance her sense of power by bringing greater distinctiveness to her work. She wanted to be a leader in her field.

- Lotus 4—Awakening Energy: Daryn wanted to have a greater understanding of the art of compassion. She was not clear how compassion could make her more powerful.

- Lotus 5—Radiance Energy: Daryn had always been fascinated by transformation and was curious about using epiphany practices.

- Lotus 6—Rapture Energy: Daryn wanted more partnership with others. She had always worked alone.

- Lotus 7—Bliss Energy: Daryn wanted to enjoy a sense of freedom in her practice and be freed of nagging chatter in her head.

To prepare for the turns, Daryn spent time working on Lotus 4, the awakening heart energy. She opened her heart to countenance the suffering she had endured as a change agent and the suffering she had witnessed in organizations. She acknowledged to herself the stress of maintaining a can-do attitude. This step was hard. Daryn had always been proud of her ability to overcome roadblocks and deliver results. The notion of accepting inadequacies and suffering was new to her. Centering in compassion, Daryn was ready for the first turn.

Turn 1—Power into Radiance. Daryn aimed to conquer her inner blocks. So she took the compulsion to conquer external roadblocks and transmuted the energy into inner illumination. For example, Daryn had noticed that, behind their can-do attitude, most Linco executives often felt vulnerable and uncertain. Daryn's usual response would have been to propose an action plan to help the executives to confront the apparent discrepancy in their leadership behavior. Instead, Daryn decided to take time to reflect on her own inner and outer behavior before she tackled the problem she saw in her clients. In confronting her own behavior, Daryn discovered she was afraid of being stuck and powerless. She feared that any display of vulnerability might hurt her credibility. Daryn wanted to be accepted as competent and professional. To face her fears and desires, Daryn turned her usual outward oriented can-do attitude into inner courage. She learned to have compassion for the trials that she and other executives had to endure. Through fearless awareness, Daryn was able to shine a light on her inner roadblocks. She even applied her sense of humor to witnessing her own hubris and pomposity.

Turn 2—Relational Concerns into Creative Partnerships. Daryn's fear of partnering was based on her feelings of inadequacy. She feared if she let down her "professional" guard, others would find her out. She found that her fear of powerlessness made her intolerant of others' weaknesses. To avoid feeling these fears, Daryn had avoided working with other consultants. She now experimented with opening herself to collaborative opportunities. Instead of saying no, she explored. Instead of waiting for invitations, she invited others to join her. Instead of intimidating others with her success, she used her success to open doors for others.

Turn 3—Consuming Concerns into the Pursuit of Bliss. Daryn dealt with her livelihood fears by reviewing her fifteen years of self-employment. Although it was never clear at the beginning of each year where the income would be coming from, she had, in fact, had a lot of paid work every year. She discovered that her economic fears constrained freedom in her practice. She had always opted for security rather than pushing the boundaries. As a result, she often felt she was not true to her own spirit or realizing her full potential. In light of this review, Daryn decided to embrace freedom and find ways to make work and spirit converge. For example, instead of being hesitant and reticent when the spiritual dimension of work came up in workplace conversations, Daryn became more open about her own interest in and learning about the topic. She learned to share more of the "nonprofessional" side of herself with others. She experimented with integrating new scientific ideas such as self-organization and the practices of compassion and epiphany in her work. The new ideas and practices helped her see her work not only as a source of income but also a source of creativity and fulfillment. She discovered that the true source of livelihood was within. It was a source that never runs dry. Daryn found that the three turns deepened her appreciation of herself, her work, and her clients. She felt a lightness of heart and a readiness to experiment. ◀

In the next application, you will see Daryn's work with OldCo, another case company.

▶ Application
OldCo's Three Turns of Transformation

Viewed as an old economy company, OldCo had seen its share value decline by 90 percent. Although OldCo remained a multi-billion-dollar business with revenue in the millions, it realized that the writing was on the wall: Transform or decline into oblivion. The executives were both excited and fearful about change. There were many skeletons in the closet, and they feared that deep change would drag them out. Multiple attempts to restructure the company had caused much suffering. The organization had become joyless. What did OldCo have to do to transform itself? Using the seven energies, Daryn helped OldCo assess how the organization had been using its creativity:

- Lotus 1—Consuming Energy: OldCo is consumed by fears of imminent demise.

- Lotus 2—Relational Energy: There is a prevalence of cliques. Instead of working together as a team, employees and management dissipate their relational energy in these cliques, where gossip and intrigue become the staples of communication.

- Lotus 3—Power Energy: Achievement energy is engaged in power struggles. The more the company talks about cross-functional collaboration, the more people become defensive about their turf.

- Lotus 4—Compassion Energy: The company feels sorry for itself. Instead of acknowledging suffering, employees alternate between self-pity and hard-heartedness toward one another.

- Lotus 5—Radiance Energy: The radiance center is closed. The company is engaged in blame. They are hostile toward success stories in the new economy. They hate financial analysts and investors who ignore the company.

- Lotus 6—Rapture Energy: OldCo is envious of others' success and feels isolated and alone.

- Lotus 7—Bliss Energy: OldCo is lost in its own fears and frenzy.

Based on the above assessment, Daryn showed OldCo how to use the Three Turns of Transformation to create change. Let's look at OldCo's three turns.

Turn 1—Converting Power Energy into Inner Light. OldCo acknowledged its passive-aggressive energy pattern. The executives learned to turn the energy inward to light up a dark and unexplored territory there. They spent time in identifying and owning the dragons of fear and desire in their various "closets." Instead of being hostile about the new economy, "cold-blooded" financial analysts, and fickle investors, they transmuted their anger, directing it toward internal fears and desires. They recognized that OldCo's past success was based on providing effective business solutions. OldCo decided to aggressively build new technology platforms in electronic commerce to meet their customers' emerging needs. The dragons to conquer were not their colleagues but their own constraints against technological innovation, superior business solutions, and imaginative and nimble mindsets for continuous adaptation.

Turn 2—Converting Relational Energy into Profitable Collaboration. Once OldCo moved beyond feeling alone and isolated, it began to discover many collaborative opportunities. OldCo was not the only company trying to adapt to the new economy. Old and new companies were taking on the challenge. And more than a few offered strategic partnerships to OldCo.

Turn 3—Converting Consuming Energy into Blissful Pursuits. Instead of being consumed by its own fears and passivity, OldCo discovered untapped bliss energy in its employees and business partners. Instead of dwelling on the glory of past successes, OldCo turned its attention to discovering new frontiers and opportunities. Using its considerable resources, OldCo started to turn an old economy dinosaur into a potential powerhouse of the new economy. ◄

Bliss can be the experience of pure play. When you are immersed in bliss, you can lose track of time. Following your bliss has long been Joseph Campbell's favorite injunction to those who are searching for the right career or the right organization focus.

▶ Application: The Bliss Trekkers

"Follow your bliss" could well be the personal and business motto of the founders of BlissTrek.com. The four original trekkers all loved technology. Immersing themselves in technology was pure play. As a result, they were very good at what they did. They had no trouble in acquiring very well-paid jobs, along with fabulous stock options. By continuing on this path, they could have settled for a very interesting and satisfying life.

However, they soon saw that the benefits of the technological revolution they were helping to create would accrue mostly to those with huge capital. Small businesses would be left out in the cold. Not able to afford the technological resources, most small business owners would not be able to participate in e-commerce easily. The trekkers decided to use their technological creativity to enable others to follow their bliss. They established BlissTrek.com to provide the tools for small organizations to create and manage their own websites and market their goods, services, and causes on the Internet. They hired Daryn to help clarify their change intention. The trekkers' Three Turns of Transformation follow.

Turn 1—Radiance. The trekkers' journey was motivated by compassion and bliss. They opened their hearts (Lotus 4) to include others, that is, small businesses, in the economy. Their compassion gave them the courage to convert the individualistic power and achievement drive of Lotus 3 into a radiant energy devoted to conquering the barriers of small businesses to participation in e-commerce.

Turn 2—Community Partnership. Through the creation of BlissTrek.com, the trekkers converted the concerns for individual legacy of Lotus 2 into energy for building an e-commerce community for small businesses.

Turn 3—Bliss. The trekkers overcame their concerns for personal survival and economic livelihood of Lotus 1 and converted the consuming energy into a pursuit of technological and commercial innovation for a larger community.

The trekkers' Three Turns of Transformation enabled them to respond quickly to emerging opportunities and to find fulfillment through service to others. ◄

Epiphanies are everyday gifts. You can now see how organizations, by using epiphany practices, can learn to tap into transcendental experiences and high-speed change energies. Exhibits 8.1 and 8.2 can be used to apply the seven energy centers of the Lotus Path and the Three Turns of Transformation in your organization.

Exhibit 8.1. Seven Energies Assessment Form

Instructions: Observe and describe how the seven energies of the Lotus Path manifest themselves in your system.

System under focus: _____

Lotus 1—Consuming energy:

Lotus 2—Relational energy:

Exhibit 8.1. Seven Energies Assessment Form, Cont'd

Lotus 3—Power energy:

Lotus 4—Compassion energy:

Lotus 5—Radiance energy:

Lotus 6—Rapture energy:

Lotus 7—Bliss energy:

Exhibit 8.2. Three Turns Worksheet

System under focus: _____

Identify the unacknowledged suffering endured by the system under focus:

Turn 1—Power concerns into radiance. Brainstorm how you can convert the power energy of Lotus 3 in your system into an illuminating light on the unacknowledged fears and desires in your system:

Turn 2—Relational concerns into creative partnerships. Brainstorm how you can convert the relational energy of Lotus 2 in your system into creative partnerships:

Turn 3—Consuming concerns into pursuit of bliss. Brainstorm how you can convert the consuming energy of Lotus 1 into blissful pursuits:

Discovery and Epiphany Tips

- Help people and organizations adjust to discovery.

- The newness of discovery can be overwhelming. The change can seem like a mirage. One moment, the boon of discovery is a lustrous treasure, and the next, it seems unreal, or sadly tarnished. One moment, people are practicing new skills and the next, they revert to the old ways. People have doubts. Then, just as quickly, joy and optimism seize them again. Reassure people that disbelief is natural and that the gifts of change are real.

- Accept skepticism. The epiphanies described in this chapter may be viewed as alien to the workplace, especially in "no-nonsense" cultures. Let the skepticism come and go. A sense of humor and a discovery attitude are helpful.

- Spread joy. Discovery is about joy and curiosity.

- Lighten up. Joy cannot be legislated.

Now that you have looked at the epiphany methods and tips, you may want to practice them by trying the following activities.

Practice Activities

1. Where do you see radiance in your organization? What brings on the radiance in your system? How can you increase the radiance in your system?

2. Identify all the ways people in your organization collaborate with each other.

3. As a change agent, who do you count as your partners? How do you support one another's work?

4. What gives you bliss in your work? Is your organization following its bliss? What is its bliss? Identify what facilitates and what blocks bliss in your organization.

5. Use the seven energy centers of the Lotus Path to assess how your organization is using its creative energy. Apply the Three Turns of Transformation to convert limited energy usage into transformative epiphanies.

Summary and Preview

In this chapter, you learned about the Discovery Cycle and the art of epiphany. I described the three epiphanies associated with discovery: radiance, rapture, and bliss. These epiphanies enable organizations to achieve targets and fulfil purpose amidst rapid change. I presented and illustrated the use of the Three Turns of Transformation, a method for converting low-level energies and concerns into high-grade energies and high-level goals.

In this chapter, you completed learning about all seven energies of the Lotus Path. These seven energies can direct a system to fulfill its highest potential. Fulfillment is the reward of transformation. In the next chapter, you will look at the Integration Cycle and use the Seven Synergy Steps to create innovations.

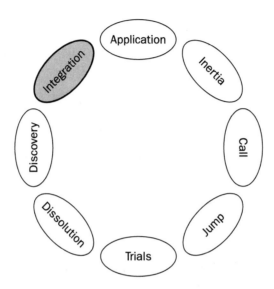

What new wholes can we create?

9

Integration and Synergy

SYNERGY MEANS COMBINING PARTS to produce something greater than the sum of those parts—a greater whole. In organizations, creating synergy is often a priority in mergers and acquisitions, partnerships, alliances, and teamwork activities. As the drive toward globalization and industry consolidation accelerates, so will the quest for synergy in organizations (McMurdy, 2000). Creating synergy is the focus of this chapter.

In the last chapter, you learned that, through discovery, a system can access high-level energy through radiance, rapture, and bliss. These three epiphanies, as they were described, can give you powerful awareness or enlightened perspectives. How do you and your organization take these perspectives and work with others who may have different orientations and experiences? In other words, how do you work with differences effectively? This is the challenge of the Integration Cycle.

In the Integration Cycle, a system combines the new/different/strange with the old/similar/familiar to create synergy. Synergy is about understanding the dynamics of whole systems (Fuller, 2000). I have designed a process called the Seven Synergy

Steps based on the work of Nancy Adler (1980), a leading contributor to the field of cross-cultural management. You will learn how practitioner Hingram uses the Seven Synergy Steps to help clients create mutually enhancing relationships. Several applications and tips on strengthening synergy capacity are presented. Now let's look at integration and synergy.

The Integration Cycle

The aim of the Integration Cycle is to intermesh the disparate energies that have been mobilized in the transformation process. In mythological tales, integration is the beginning of the return journey. The adventurers have discovered the gifts of their quests and must now return to their old communities. Before arriving home, the adventurers are given more tasks at the portal of re-entry. They have to find ways to combine their newfound gifts with the offers of others to create a mutually enhancing community.

The Integration Cycle poses several challenges to changing organizations. The first is *incorporating the gifts of discovery* to create a new pattern of self-organization. In organizations, these gifts of change can include new visions, missions, and goals. New inventions must be tested. Newfound markets must be developed. New recruits to the organization have to be properly oriented. To ensure that you profit from the fruits of change, you want to manage the Integration Cycle with respect and sensitivity.

The second challenge is *reconciling differences.* The journey of change attracts a great diversity of ideas, people, situations, and norms. The new and strange mix can be a source of stress and strife. Innovations may clash and immobilize the energies that have emerged. You have to find ways for the different elements to work together.

The third challenge is *sustaining the system* emerging from the change journey. This new emergent system is in a fragile state and can easily be overwhelmed by the pull of tradition and familiar habits. You want to provide delicate care to ensure its survival.

The last challenge is *creating a new vision* that befits the newly emergent entity. New possibilities are created when different enterprises or teams merge to become one. To capture and focus these emergent possibilities, you want to create a vision that will open minds to new horizons. The new vision can then direct the diverse energies in the new entity toward shared goals and futures.

Bringing together people, cultures, and ideas can generate stress and strife. To meet the challenges of the Integration Cycle, you want to be skillful in facilitating synergy. Before looking at the actual steps in facilitating synergy, let's look further at synergy.

What Is Synergy?

I define synergy as energies coming together to produce something whole that is different from or more desirable than the sum of its constituent parts. A simple example is when 1 + 1 = 3+. When bees and flowers make contact, the meeting eventually produces fruit, more flowers, more bees, honey, and so on. When humans group together, they produce cultures, histories, and civilizations. Synergy is a process that helps to re-create the world in a richer form. Synergy is integral to creativity and change.

Synergy is at once simple and complex. We experience it in ourselves. We see it everywhere. We can point to examples. But we cannot say, definitively, "Here it is; this is synergy." We know synergy as we know life, through continuing experience and our expanding capacities. Organizations are created through the synergy of people, material, and technology.

Because part of the process occurs in a "black box," synergy is a mystery. This black box is the great mystery of spiritual and creative experience. You come to know synergy through experiential intelligence rather than from intellectual intelligence. You cannot always explain it or attach meaning to it. There is a charming story about the Buddha holding up a flower as the answer to many complex questions (Osbon, 1991). Synergy is a flower. Synergy is a bird. Synergy is life. What is the meaning of a flower, a bird, or of life? We may understand all the constituent parts of a flower, its biology, chemistry, physics, and its social history, but we may never be able to answer the how and why of a flower. The exquisite beauty of the lotus flower or a rose cannot be reduced to its separate petals. Synergy invites openness.

Synergy is the process of becoming whole. It is a process in which constituent parts (or solitary wholes) come together to form a new whole or system. The newly formed system continues, in turn, to interact with other intelligent systems to bring yet another reality into being. Synergy is thus like a dance of time and eternity.

Synergy is a natural way of the Tao. It is inherent in all things. It is formless, yet it takes myriad forms. It is the intelligence that transforms relationships and reality. Synergy is archetypal creativity (Lao Zi, 1998).

Synergy simplifies and creates complexity. Synergy simplifies because it unites disparate parts into a new whole. Synergy leads to complexity because the process involves separating wholes into their distinct parts and recombining them to form new relationships, within new wholes. Thus synergy is part of change.

Synergy can be thought of as an invisible glue that links apparent solitary entities into a whole system. The synergy process involves reconfiguring relational links within and across distinct intelligent systems. Previously unconnected solitudes now reference each other in their functioning. The cross-references serve to coordinate the activities of the parts (or what we used to think of as parts) toward some shared purpose. The new referential links or relationships may not be visible or measurable. Synergistic connection is integral to the science of wholeness (Peat, 1991).

Synergy is a story of co-transformation and co-creation. In synergy, systems shift boundaries and consciousness. They reference each other through constant adjustment and feedback. By amplifying differences continuously, disparate systems bring forth new shared realities.

To conclude, synergy is key to change and creativity. As such, working with synergy is integral to facilitating organization change. In the box below, you will find an action check list for a synergy facilitator. After that, you will look at the practical steps in facilitating synergy and applications of these steps in organizations.

A Synergy Facilitator. . .

- ☐ Helps himself or herself and others to become culturally self-aware.
- ☐ Appreciates and respects similarities and differences.
- ☐ Finds common ground.
- ☐ Creates shared goals.
- ☐ Supports ambiguity and uncertainty.
- ☐ Seeks diversity as a source of new energies.
- ☐ Recognizes blocks and obstacles to synergy.
- ☐ Facilitates the innovation of new possibilities.

The Dance of Synergy

Synergy is a dance of creativity. I designed the Seven Synergy Steps based on the work of Nancy Adler (1980). Following is a summary of the steps, which are also illustrated in Figure 9.1.

1. Attract solitudes.
2. Create common ground.
3. Accentuate distinctiveness.
4. Remove blocks and dissolve boundaries.
5. Proliferate resources.
6. Journey into the unknown.
7. Create new possibilities.

Figure 9.1. Seven Synergy Steps

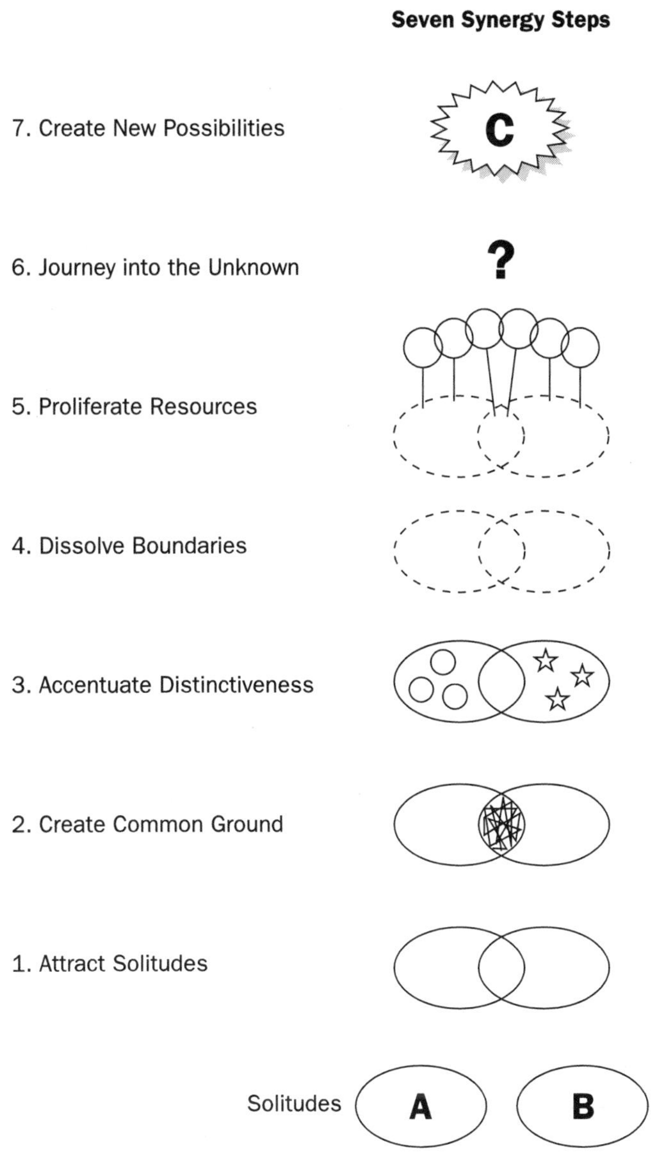

Seven Synergy Steps

7. Create New Possibilities

6. Journey into the Unknown

5. Proliferate Resources

4. Dissolve Boundaries

3. Accentuate Distinctiveness

2. Create Common Ground

1. Attract Solitudes

Solitudes

Adapted in part from Cultural Synergy: The Management of Cross-Cultural Organizations by Nancy Adler (1980). In W.W. Burke & L.D. Goodstein (Eds.), *Trends and Issues in OD*. San Francisco: Jossey-Bass/Pfeiffer. Used with permission.

Like a dance, these steps are flow states or experiential qualities, rather than mechanical movements. However, to help in understanding the transformation process, I will describe each of the steps or flow states as if it were a frozen frame of a process.

I will describe the basic steps as they apply to creating synergy from two separate energies or systems. Later, you will look at applications in multiple systems. In describing the steps below, I will use A and B to represent the two different systems. The systems can be different cultures (such as arrow and spiral), organizations, units, teams, individuals, or aspects of a single individual.

Step 1. Attract Solitudes

Synergy is a process of co-transformation or co-creation. A condition for co-transformation is a chance for intelligent systems to interact. The first step is therefore to attract and connect with co-transformers or co-creators in your environment. This often means connecting with the culture, group, unit, or person that you are working with. In other words, the presence of synergy conditions will give rise to intent to transform. Or vice versa.

In this step, A and B acknowledge and accept each other as co-transformers. This may be difficult, though. We often see people within our systems as the greatest obstacles to our transformation. But assuming (perhaps rashly) there are no mistakes in the universe, the systems that are right next to you are the ones you need for transformation. Similarly, the energy and intelligence we need to transform our global human system are already on the planet. In the same way, what a person needs in order to grow already exists within him or her. It is the lack of self-awareness and acceptance that blocks out what a system needs most.

In accepting each other, each system is altering its relationship with its own environment (A and B are in each other's environments). This step also alters how each references the other. For example, A and B can move from indifference to a dance partnership.

Step 2. Create Common Ground

After accepting each other as co-transformers, A and B will go through a process of identifying what they have in common (the areas that overlap) and what they have that is unique to each. This is akin to stocktaking among partners. The stocktaking process reconciles A and B to each other. They become more knowledgeable about and appreciative of each other as whole systems. They have an appreciative awareness of the strengths and weaknesses they bring to the table. Finding common ground is a key goal of the Future Search change approach (Weisbord & Janoff, 1995). Finding common ground enables us to shape our collective future.

Common ground or similarities come in many forms. The important thing here is to maximize the areas of commonality. Below is a sample list of categories that A and B could have in common:

Location A and B are co-located in the same geographical space; they share an office, neighborhood, community, region, ecological system, and so on.

Affiliation They belong to the same team, organization, or institution.

Identity They share the same affinity-group membership.

Interest They both have similar interests.

Goals They share common goals of improvement, adventure, and so on.

Step 3: Accentuate Distinctiveness

After the search for common ground comes the identification of uniqueness. What do A and B bring to the table? What does each have to offer? What makes A different or distinct? What makes B different or distinct? The important thing here is to focus on the distinctiveness. There are many dimensions of distinctiveness, including physical, social, or psychological characteristics; affiliations; talents; skills; concerns; gripes; stereotypes; perceptions; definitions of situations; material and social resources; desires; interests; goals; objectives; histories; experiences; styles; preferences; and circumstances.

It is important to note that when commonalities and differences are ignored, A and B may struggle for dominance and recognition. Or they may withdraw, interacting around a narrow ground of compromise.

With the recognition of commonalities and differences, A and B can now prepare for a common future. They have joined forces. Although A and B are still conscious of their own distinct identities, they are now acting together as a unit. A new kind of consciousness emerges. The boundary that separated them before is now a meeting place.

Step 4. Dissolve Boundaries

The distinct identities of A and B before the merger now have to be dissolved or redefined. They must now embark on a common course. They begin to think of a common identity. The common stock they own is now viewed as their common potential.

Step 5. Proliferate Resources

You create new resources or data pools by highlighting the following: The overlap of A and B; A's distinctiveness; and B's distinctiveness.

As you can see in Figure 9.1, from two circles (A and B) coming together, we now have three or more circles, representing new data pools or resource bases. These new circles become their joint database. The pool of commonalities and differences may contain a large number of items. Select only the most critical to the co-transformation. Following are some examples of new data pools or resource bases:

- A's technical talent pool

- B's financial talent pool

- A's market

- B's market

- A's products and services

- B's marketing expertise

- A's management experience

- B's flexible culture

Step 6. Journey into the Unknown

A new database is created. Now a journey into the unknown of synergy begins. Maximize the interaction of the proliferated circles. Facilitate critical exchanges. Study them from new perspectives. Appreciate them. Stare at them. Wonder at them. What could arise from this pool of resources or possibilities? Wait. Accept. Remain open. Anticipate the reincarnation. Let things happen.

The journey into the unknown is likely filled with chaos. The proliferation of resources is a fragmenting process. The integrity of A and B are both redefined. This is the "between" stage (Sambhava, 1994). This is the gap, the black box of transformation, the void to which we must all yield. This is the Dissolution Cycle of the Archetypal Change Journey. The old identities are dissolving; the common and new ones are not yet born. A and B can easily revert to the struggle for compromise or domination.

Step 7. Create New Possibilities

Given the new data or resource base, what can be created from that? What can be innovated? Meditate. Wait. Give the new time to emerge. Let the new form morph into being. This is the process of emergence or incarnation. C, the new reality, is the synthesis of A and B. C is the synergy. It is the realization of the deep potential in A and B. Synergy is possible because the coming together dissolves the rigidity of the old boundaries. When the energy within the boundary is released and is channeled, synergy is possible.

Synergy is magical. As change agents, we work in the realm of mystery, never knowing for sure how things will unfold. Through trust, faith, and skill, we can participate in the mystery of cultural transformation and synergy.

What emerges from the transformation process will not always be seen as innovative, good, or desirable. This emergent product of synergy often stays hidden or, if revealed, can even repel. What was supposed to be a new swan looks like an ugly duckling. The system from which it emerges is more likely to reject it. Often, only a few recognize the potential of the new and take the risk of championing it. This championing role is the task of change agents.

The same principles and steps can apply to multiple systems. The steps involve a basic movement of resolution and dissolution, coming together and falling apart. By performing these basic movements or basic rules, systems can co-create new realities with multiple partners. To apply the Seven Synergy Steps, use the Synergy Quiz (Exhibit 9.1) as a guide and follow the steps illustrated in Figure 9.1. The practical applications in the next section will give you more ideas on using the synergy steps.

Exhibit 9.1. Synergy Quiz

Step 1. Attract Solitudes

- Who and what are the unconnected solitudes within and outside of your system?

- What are the key characteristics of these solitudes?

Step 2. Search for Common Ground

- What are the commonalities or similarities among the solitudes?

- How can these commonalities and similarities serve as common ground and building blocks for synergy?

Exhibit 9.1. Synergy Quiz, Cont'd

Step 3. Accentuate Distinctiveness

· What are the distinctive differences of each of the solitudes?

Step 4. Dissolve Boundaries

· What are the barriers to synergy in your system?

· How are these barriers maintained?

· What is the cost of maintaining these barriers?

· Who can remove these barriers?

· What strategies will remove these barriers?

Step 5. Proliferate Resources

· What new values can be created from the participants' commonalities?

· What new values can be created from the distinctive differences of the participants?

· What new platform can be built on the commonalities and differences?

Step 6. Journey into the Unknown

· What is the new frontier for your system?

· Where is the jumping-off point for your system?

Exhibit 9.1. Synergy Quiz, Cont'd

- What must your system let go of to take on a new journey?

- What are the fears associated with synergy?

- What strategies can help the system overcome those fears?

Step 7. Create New Possibilities

- What has been birthing in your system?

- What excites your system?

- What future is desired?

- What are people in awe of?

- What does the Promised Land look like?

- What can change agents do to help bring forth the desired new reality?

The three applications we'll look at next are about creating synergy in TCom. You may recall from Chapters Two and Seven that the lack of synergy is an issue within TCom management. In Applications 1 and 2, you'll look at how practitioner Hingram facilitates Synergy Dialogues with CEO Arthur Jay (AJ) and his managers. In Application 3, you'll look at how AJ and the practitioners facilitate a Synergy Symposium with TCom's acquired company, ShenkiCo.

▶ Application: Synergy Dialogues, Part I

Bjorn had high expectations when he answered AJ's invitation to join TCom. They each brought qualities and capacities that were the ingredients for fantastic synergy. But after a year, Bjorn and AJ's relationship deteriorated and was a source of frustration for both. They were in danger of falling out as colleagues and as friends. The impaired relationship affected the whole organization. Using synergy steps, Hingram facilitated a series of Synergy Dialogues to help Bjorn and AJ review the patterns of their relationship. Following is a summary of Bjorn and AJ's Seven Synergy Steps.

Step 1. Attract Solitudes. They were thrilled with the prospect of working together to build something fabulous. They had the right conditions for synergy.

Step 2. Create Common Ground. They were particularly surprised by their relational impasse, given that they were in the same profession and enjoyed one another's humor. But the common ground was dominated by the fact that they also had a hierarchical relationship. AJ was Bjorn's boss. They did not contract with each other on how they would manage their new common ground. As a result, the unspoken expectations never surfaced to be dealt with. They were often at cross-purposes—Bjorn expected AJ to be boss whereas AJ looked for the understanding of a friend. They now recognized that their common ground included a reporting relationship, friendship, professional affiliation, and fellow adventurers' camaraderie.

Step 3. Accentuate Distinctiveness. Because they were friends and in the same profession, their differences were never articulated. They did not accentuate what was distinct about them to capitalize on the differences. Instead, they were surprised, shocked, and angered by the differences. They now recognized that their differences included cultural background, personality style, pacing, their approaches to decision making and risk taking, and family status.

Step 4. Dissolve Boundaries. Due to inadequate exploration of common ground and differences, Bjorn and AJ, in essence, remained two solitudes that shared the same organization. The solitudes functioned as opposing polarities, dancing out of step. They now recognized that they wanted to open themselves to partnership.

Step 5. Proliferate Resources. Because of the lack of a contract on common ground and acknowledgement of differences, they had worked alongside rather than with each other. To realize their synergy potential, they brainstormed on a range of resources they could create from their differences and commonalities. Some of these included exploring leadership beyond functional expertise, creating a dynamic and diverse global enterprise, learning about planning and financial management, fundraising, and regional contacts.

Step 6. Journey into the Unknown. The unknown was a new frontier in their relationship—how to be both friends and boss and subordinate. Another unknown aspect was how the two men would evolve their bilateral relationship in the context of a multilateral team. To create a gap for the emergence of new patterns, Bjorn and AJ decided to hold the Synergy Dialogue over a number of sessions. This arrangement recognized that what contributed to problems in their relationship was the lack of continuing dialogue. The lack of dialogue was caused by the erroneous assumption that they already knew each other well.

Step 7. Create New Possibilities. By exploring the unknown over a period of time, they were in effect establishing a new pattern. Bjorn and AJ learned to cultivate a work partnership that allowed them to create greater synergy. The work synergy in turn enhanced their friendship and reporting relationship. ◀

Exhibit 9.2 summarizes the key steps in AJ and Bjorn's Synergy Dialogue. Exhibit 9.3 is a blank Synergy Form representing a simplified version of the Seven Synergy Steps that you can use as a worksheet in facilitating Synergy Dialogues.

Exhibit 9.2. Sample Synergy Form

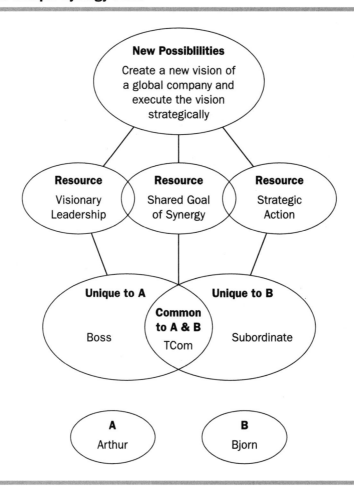

Exhibit 9.3. Synergy Form

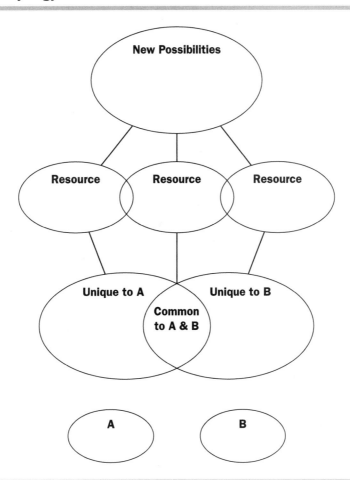

By using the synergy steps as a template, individuals can look back at their synergy process to uncover what went wrong and how to put things right. In the next application, you will see how AJ applies lessons learned from the Synergy Dialogues to his next hire.

▶ Application: Synergy Dialogues, Part II

Kamah was hired in the fourth year of AJ's tenure as CEO. By then, AJ had become more conscious about creating a diversity advantage through synergy. Through his work with Hingram, AJ had learned about the Confucian principle of Ren, a Chinese character made up of the root words "upright person" and "two," which together means the ethics of harmonious relationship or relational ethics (Allen, 1997). Hingram defined Ren as the radiance and transcendence of energies in harmony (see Figure 9.2). AJ wanted to inform his leadership with Ren. He conscientiously applied the synergy steps to create beneficial relationships with new hires and with his team.

Figure 9.2. Ren—Relational Ethics

Step 1. Attract Solitudes. AJ was very clear about what was needed to make his team great. He wanted to attract a leader who could help him create synergy out of diversity. He was disciplined and vigorous in his search. He invited managers and employees to identify what talents were needed for synergy. The key talent identified was the skill of focusing diversity and facilitating synergy. AJ was guided by clear synergy intent. Kamah brought a multidisciplinary background and had a track record of building and facilitating multicultural teams. She was thrilled with the prospect of using her diversity experience and skills to help expand a global enterprise.

Step 2. Create Common Ground. There was a common ground on Kamah's hiring. Kamah, AJ, and the team all wanted to create a synergistic organization to maximize creativity and innovation. A week after Kamah was hired, she participated in a week-long retreat with the whole executive team during which they had candid conversations about visions and expectations. The team members agreed to adopt the actions of a synergy facilitator (see "A Synergy Facilitator" on page 170).

Step 3. Accentuate Distinctiveness. Kamah, AJ, and the team identified individual uniquenesses. For example, AJ's leadership was visionary and charismatic. Bjorn was bold in executing strategies. Other team members brought world-class expertise in several disciplines. Kamah brought a multidisciplinary background and diversity skills and experience.

Step 4. Dissolve Boundaries. To welcome Kamah into the team, Hingram facilitated an inclusion process. The group members identified what constitutes inclusive and exclusive behavior and norms. They brainstormed ways to maintain an open and inclusive team climate.

Step 5. Proliferate Resources. The team identified how commonalities and differences could add value to the organization. For example, the team's synergy experience could become a database for TCom and Linco. AJ could use his visionary charisma to attract greater diversity into the management ranks of TCom and Linco. Kamah could help TCom build more collaborative relationships with its offshore operations.

Step 6. Journey into the Unknown. Kamah, AJ, and the team agreed to accept the uncertainty of their collective partnership. They agreed to support each other in their group and individual change journeys.

Step 7. Create New Possibilities. Kamah, AJ, and the team decided to adopt and adapt the Synergy Dialogues for themselves as well as for their employee teams. They set a goal of helping each employee to develop and use the Synergy Steps. They also wanted to hold a Synergy Symposium with ShenkiCo, TCom's offshore company. ◀

In the above applications, we see that, once an individual starts using the synergy process, he or she can improve synergy for the whole group. In the next application, we look at how AJ and the practitioners facilitate a Synergy Symposium to promote synergy with TCom's acquired company.

We saw in Chapters Two and Seven that TCom and its acquired offshore company, ShenkiCo, struggled over control and the "us and them" mentality. AJ requested the help of HR manager Julee and practitioners Hingram, Daryn, and Arente. Using synergy steps as a design template, the practitioners organized a Synergy Symposium to explore synergy and to search for desired futures. Following are the key elements of the symposium design.

▶ Application: Synergy Symposium

An organizing council was formed with participants from different parts of the two organizations. The Seven Synergy Steps were used as a design framework for the content and the process of the symposium. At the symposium, AJ and Taag, president of ShenkiCo, explained the purpose of the symposium and their commitment to common goals. The organizing council presented the Seven Synergy Steps. AJ and Bjorn briefly described their personal experiences with the steps.

Participants self-selected themselves into seven subgroups, with each subgroup representing one of the Seven Synergy Steps. In forming the subgroups, participants were encouraged to reflect a variety of differences, including gender, culture, region, rank, and discipline in their group membership. The task of each subgroup was to design and facilitate a learning module on its particular synergy step for the whole assembly. Using the Synergy Quiz as a guide, each subgroup worked with its particular step.

Each of the seven subgroups then came back to the large group and facilitated a ninety-minute learning session on synergy, using Steps 1 through 7. The seven sessions made up the symposium content and process.

As a concluding activity, the whole group acted out the Seven Synergy Steps:

1. Isolated solitudes connecting. Carefully avoiding eye contact, participants spread out in a random fashion in the room to symbolize isolated solitudes. After some minutes, participants moved toward one another to make contact.

2. Isolated solitudes created common ground by forming a circle. The space in the center represented the common ground.

3. Individuals and groups came forward to tell of their distinctive differences.

4. Individuals and groups removed blocks and barriers to synergy.

5. Individuals and groups formed clusters representing multiple resources.

6. The whole group stayed still and silent for three minutes to signify a gap or the unknown in the change journey.

7. The group celebrated the Synergy Symposium by reading agreed-on goals and actions. ◀

Following is a summary of the key actions in facilitating a Synergy Symposium.

Facilitating a Synergy Symposium

- Form an organizing council (OC) with participants from the different partnering organizations, teams, or units.

- OC coordinates symposium logistics.

- At the symposium, OC presents the Seven Synergy Steps, with testimonials from people who have used the Seven Synergy Steps. OC hands out Synergy Quiz to each participant.

- Symposium participants work in seven subgroups, with each subgroup focusing on one synergy step.

- Each of the seven subgroups facilitates a learning session for the whole assembly on a synergy step, starting from Step 1 through Step 7.

- To conclude the symposium, the whole group acts out the Seven Synergy Steps.

A sample of the Seven Synergy Steps played out in ShenkiCo and TCom's symposium follows:

Step 1. Attract Solitudes. ShenkiCo and TCom came together through a friendly takeover.

Step 2. Search for Common Ground. Both companies were in the same business with expertise in international operations. They were both adept at using technology to create new value. They embarked on a shared destiny.

Step 3. Accentuate Distinctiveness. TCom culture emphasized arrow qualities such as aggressiveness and quick action. ShenkiCo culture valued deep thinking and strategic moves. TCom had deeper pockets. ShenkiCo had unique experience with the offshore assets. TCom was more functionally oriented, and ShenkiCo was more environmentally conscious.

Step 4. Remove Blocks and Dissolve Boundaries. The group identified a key barrier to synergy as the lack of attention to the cultural and the human side of merging. Time and money were focused on merging in the areas of finance, computer use, and furniture. The group wanted to link culture and mindset to forge an expanded vision of the combined company. They acknowledged excitement, anger, sadness, and burnout from the merger.

Step 5. Proliferate Resources. Based on their stocktaking during Step 2, the group brainstormed new resources they could co-create. For example, they wanted to combine their respective strengths in arrow and spiral competencies to create a more flexible culture and a broader skill set. The flexibility and breadth could enhance their creativity and improve their responsiveness to changing conditions.

Step 6. Journey into the Unknown. They decided that one way of creating a gap to help the new to emerge was to adopt a rule called "count five." The idea was that, when presented with a situation, a problem, or idea in meetings, they would silently count to five before responding so as to lessen the likelihood of voicing ill-considered judgments, advice, or stereotypes.

Step 7. Create New Possibilities. The group envisioned itself becoming a global enterprise powered by synergistic cultures and strategies.

The above applications show how the synergy steps were used in TCom. These steps can be used with individuals and groups to improve relationships and enhance innovations. Exhibit 9.4 is a worksheet that can help you apply the Seven Synergy Steps in your organization.

Exhibit 9.4. Synergy Worksheet

Step 1. Attract Solitudes. Identify the solitudes:

Step 2. Create Common Ground. What can serve as common ground?

Step 3. Accentuate Distinctiveness. List the distinctiveness of each of the solitudes:

Step 4. Dissolve Boundaries. Identify the boundaries to be dissolved:

Step 5. Proliferate Resources. Brainstorm new resources that can be created from the commonalities and differences of the synergy partners:

Step 6. Journey into the Unknown. Where/what is the unknown? What can serve as the jumping-off point?

Step 7. Create New Possibilities. What is the desired future?

Our growing multicultural human system invites increased synergy capacity. The following are some suggestions on how change agents can enhance their capacity to facilitate synergy.

Tips on Developing Synergy Capacity

- Synergy responds to awareness. Direct appreciative awareness on how and why systems work.

- Appreciative awareness is to attend a system with loving kindness and positive anticipation. When you work with a team of diverse cultures, you want to pay appreciative attention to the synergy potential in the team. By so doing, you can gently bring forth synergy.

- You can also facilitate synergy by meditating on wholeness, the totality of a person, group, or organization. Imagine a circle to represent the wholeness of a system. Meditate on the vitality of the system. By focusing your appreciative awareness on this circle, you can help bring forth the synergy within. When this is done in a large group of people, the power of the exercise is multiplied greatly.

- Practice awe and wonder, which are not usually included in the toolbox of change agents, yet are powerful approaches to change. Awe is respectful amazement. Wonder is admiring with joyful gratitude. They are proper attitudes for working with human systems.

- Participate in wholeness. The global human system is a complex web of energies and rich potential. Viewed as constituent parts one at a time, there are simply too many parts that are not working. When the system is viewed as a whole, you arrive at wonder and awe.

Practice Activities

1. What are some synergy examples in your organization?
2. Identify two separate units in your organization and show how they can create synergy with each other by using the Seven Synergy Steps.

Summary and Preview

This chapter explored the challenges of the Integration Cycle in transformation. Incorporating diversity and creating synergy are key tasks. The key qualities of synergy were described and I explained how you can apply the Seven Synergy Steps to create innovations in practical situations. I listed suggestions to help change agents enhance their synergy capacities. Through integration and synergy, you can ensure that the newfound energies from the change journey are used creatively.

The next chapter will focus on the Application Cycle and enacting new patterns. You will learn the Circles Process and Sacred Canopy methods for building community in organizations.

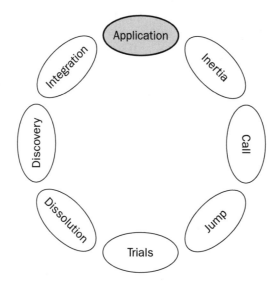

How will you use the gifts of change to benefit a larger community?

(10)

Application
and Community

ON THE GLOBAL INFORMATION AGE, change agents and their organizations have many opportunities to apply creative ideas and work toward a prosperous and healthy community. In this chapter, you will look at key challenges of the Application Cycle and practices that facilitate community.

The Application Cycle is concerned with disseminating insights and innovations gained from the change journey into a larger community. I use the term community to mean a sphere of belonging and responsibility within or outside of organizations. Application moves you from private discovery to community action. The operation can take you from your own back yard to the other side of the world. Community action raises social, political, and ethical considerations (Adler & Bird, 1988). I present two methods, Sacred Canopy (adapted from Driedger, 1996) and Circles Process (Allen, 1994), and show you how to use them to facilitate the creation of community. First, let's explore the Application Cycle.

The Application Cycle

In the previous cycles of the Archetypal Change Journey, you learned how to gain insights and synergies for yourself or your organization. In the Application Cycle, your challenge is implementing these gains to create a new way of being. The Application Cycle enables you to spread innovations to a broader audience.

In mythological tales, application is when the returned adventurers try to contribute to a new way of life by converting discoveries into practical strategies. From the Lotus Path perspective, this means applying radiance, rapture, and bliss energies (Lotuses 5, 6, 7) to deal with concerns of power, relations, and economic survival (Lotuses 3, 2, 1) in the practical world. This descent from the upper lotuses to the lower lotuses is a journey of compassion. The enlightened ones, instead of remaining in transcendence, will, out of compassion (Lotus 4), return to share new insights and improve the lot of everyday mortals. The return to serve the practical world is the essence of the Buddha story (Campbell, 1993).

In organizations, application is about bringing new business models, services, or products to market or living out a new vision and culture. When change agents bring discoveries to the practical world, they can encounter many challenges.

The first challenge is *facing skepticism and indifference.* The enlightened change agents may soon discover that their enthusiasm for change and new ideas is not matched by others. To deal with the cold reception, change agents have to recognize that other people have also been on transformation journeys. They, too, have interesting stories to tell. Therefore, if you want openness from others, be open to others' experiences.

The second challenge is *recognizing the universal worth of your innovations.* When you are in the throes of change, you may not recognize the universal significance of your unique experiences and discoveries. To complete a change journey, step back from your immersion in these new perceptions and assess how your innovations can be properly applied to benefit the larger community, to properly recognize the universal applications of your unique discoveries.

The third challenge is *converting insights into practice.* For epiphanies to benefit a system, they must be translated into practical action. This translation involves descending from the heights of imagination and transcendence and returning to everyday reality. For example, it is not enough for Julee, Arthur Jay, or Daryn to embrace empowering insights. They must use their insights in actual practice.

The fourth challenge is *eliciting support from others*. To spread the innovations from change journeys, recruit supporters from a broader community. Pioneers and early champions have to begin explaining and broadcasting their visions to those who were not on their journey. The highs and lows of the dot-com phenomenon show how ephemeral startups can be. The long-term viability of discoveries and synergies requires systemic adoption and support. Devote resources, therefore, to involve the whole system.

The fifth challenge is *adapting to diversity*. The Application Cycle is about the few communicating to the many. If diverse stakeholders are not on board, widespread implementation of the unique discoveries from the journey will not happen. This means that you have to know the needs and interests of diverse stakeholders so that you can gear your innovations and discoveries to this broad constituency.

The sixth challenge is *having the courage to exercise freedom*. That means living out your new visions and insights. It involves aligning your actions with authentic purposes, rather than with fears and desires. The ability to apply this freedom requires a skillful balance of weighing your individual needs with the community's universal concerns.

The following practices will enable you to meet the above challenges, balancing individual and community interests.

Community Practices

Community practices refer to principles and actions that facilitate connection and shared goals among diverse participants in organizations. Community can be envisioned as a web of interrelationships through which individuals can co-create meaning and futures. In the global information age, many trends are at work to reshape our thinking and practice around the concept of community. The following is a list of trends that will challenge change agents to think creatively about community building.

Trends Affecting Community Building
- Interest-based community, enabled by technology
- Burgeoning gap between rich and poor
- Transitory and ephemeral gatherings

- Transient systems participants

- Geographically dispersed teams and organizations

- Virtuality and interconnectivity

- Disembodied cyberspace interaction

- Proliferation of cybersocieties and cybernations

The interlinking of our global human system invites us to expand our perception of community. Seven practices that can facilitate inclusive community are described below. Later, we will look at methods for using them.

Practice 1. Use Open Process. To acknowledge multiple change journeys in your organization, adopt an open change process that provides continuous entry points to include people when they are ready. Stipulating few but clear guidelines, an open process can encourage flexibility and enhance inclusion.

Practice 2. Create Shared Culture. The forces of globalization simultaneously fragment traditional groupings and inter-link disparate people across boundaries. The affiliations and gatherings can be transitory though. The interactions can be highly fluid and fleeting. To foster a sense of community, change agents can help individuals develop comfort and skills to better share with and learn from diverse groups.

Practice 3. Create Anchors. Community can affirm both individuality and connectivity. When all things are volatile and constantly shifting, people need supportive anchors to stay centered. Change agents can help their organizations identify and fortify anchoring supports. These supports can include identity, culture, history, shared goals, or core competencies.

Practice 4. Put Diversity to Work. Today's organizations intermesh cultures, time zones, and interests. Change agents want to create a sense of community among diverse stakeholders by fostering collaborative processes and skills. The Synergy Symposium discussed in Chapter Nine is a useful collaborative method.

Practice 5. Foster Responsible Freedom. Responsible freedom means holding oneself accountable for actions and choices. A vibrant community thrives on creative freedom and an ethic of care (Gilligan, 1982). One way to foster a vibrant community is to increase awareness of the karmic effect of fears and desires. Methods that help you work with fears and desires such as those described in the Trials Cycle are useful in balancing individual freedom with community care.

Practice 6. Co-Create Heritage. A living system grows by referring back to its past processes or heritage. This is called self-reference (Maturana & Varela, 1992). By referencing its own past, a community fashions an informed present and brings forward a conscious new future. Continual self-reference can enable a community to preserve its essential identity while adapting to flux and complexity (Morgan, 1986). As change agents, we can enhance a system's ability to create community by helping it to look back at its own journeys. The Journey Mapping techniques in the Call Cycle are useful for self-reference.

Practice 7. Enhance Mutual Renewal. Fostering a mutually beneficial relationship between unique individuals and the larger system can enhance the renewal of both. It takes a delicate balance though. Community traditions shape individual development. In turn, individuals contribute to community renewal through innovations. Individual action prompted by fears and desires can wreak havoc in the community. On the other hand, community traditions, if applied oppressively, can stunt individual creativity. When individual potential is frozen, the community becomes a wasteland (Eliot, 1986). However, when individuals are awake to their own creative energy, undistorted by fears and desires, the community wasteland is transformed (Campbell, 1993). Thus, the practice of community links back to awakening, completing the circle of transformation.

We have looked at application challenges and at practices that facilitate community. In the next section, we will look at two methods for putting these practices into use. First, I'll present the Circles Process and its adaptations and applications.

Circles Process

The Circles Process (shown in Figure 10.1) is based on four actions associated with the circle archetype (Jung, 1969). These actions balance autonomy with interdependence. The circle symbolizes the mysterious relationship between individuals and their surrounding environment—be it work unit, organization, or society. Descriptions of these four actions follow.

Figure 10.1. Circles Process

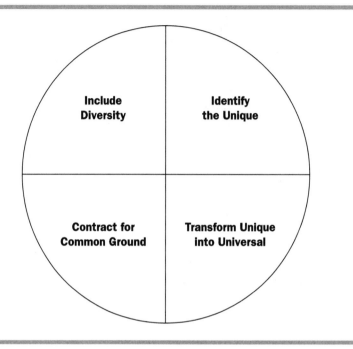

Step 1. Include Diversity

Diversity is a critical element in creating and sustaining a self-organizing community. Diversity introduces creative tension into a system. The tension creates disequilibrium and stimulates a system to self-organize innovative adaptations.
Through creative exchanges (Olson & Eoyang, 2001), participants in community
are able to contribute to and receive new resources from the environment. Creative
exchange is the essence of a thriving self-organizing system. Here are some ideas
on increasing and including diversity:

- Make inclusion a systemic practice in all transactions. Inclusion is something
  we have to do consciously. Do not assume that what you've always done will
  suit all people.

- Attract diversity from the environment by maintaining an open boundary.

- Amplify existing diversity in the system by developing a culture that values
  diversity.

- Encourage diversity learning.
- Demonstrate diversity appreciation through concrete policies and actions. Reward practices that value diversity.

Step 2. Create Common Ground

The common ground of a circle is the open space within and without. When a collection of disparate individuals comes together in a circle, a common open space is created in its midst. The act of sharing a common open space transforms a disparate group into a community. By coming together in a circle, people are using the unique presence of their bodies to define and claim an otherwise amorphous space. The defining and claiming process generates meaning and value (Albrecht & Brewer, 1990). The shared space both within and without the circle is now made sacred or meaningful to the group.

The actions also activate mental energies to stimulate the emergence of open space within our minds. As we form communal space through our bodies, we are also creating communal space within our minds. The creation of common ground affirms the ground for our individual and collective beings.

The common ground can be physical, like a region or an actual piece of land. It can represent common interest or purpose. It can be symbolic, like shared language, culture, history, or values. The common ground serves as a mutual reference point. It is a centering anchor to which individuals from different parts of the community relate. The common ground is also a symbolic garden of communal talents and aspirations. Individuals contribute to the garden and draw on it for sustenance. The de-centering and re-centering techniques described in Chapter Three are based on the above concepts. Here are some tips on creating common ground:

- Identify commonalities at multiple levels, emphasizing shared benefits.
- Create simple ground rules to facilitate complex interactions.
- Sustain and renew common ground through ongoing conversations.
- Attend to the common ground, as you would a village common.
- Build on the diversity within; recruit diversity from without. The greater the diversity, the richer the common ground.
- Mark common ground as "sacred" or "meaningful" through rituals or symbols. For example, TCom's common is an aquarium filled with tropical fish.

Different teams have their own fish in the common. A picture of the common aquarium greets visitors to their intranet site.

- Create multiple platforms for communal interaction. Create a dense web of relationships and communications via an imaginative use of technology. For example, TCom has an idea marketplace called IMart on its intranet. Work teams and units can set up their own "exhibition booths" where they showcase and shop for ideas and communicate work progress.

Step 3. Identify the Unique

The third action in community building is to identify, accentuate, and nurture unique differences. Encourage participants to value their self-awareness so that they can tune in to the unique impulses within themselves and have enough trust to voice their unique experiences and views. The aim here is to actively utilize the diversity in the community.

Identifying uniqueness helps participants in the system to tune in to the fear and desire energies that preoccupy them. The uniqueness generates the diversity needed for disequilibrium and adaptive bifurcation (as discussed in the Trials and Dissolution Cycles). The uniqueness also constitutes the raw ingredients needed to generate universal resources for the community (see the next step). Some guidelines in identifying uniqueness follow:

- Disengage the censor and judge.
- Become aware of unique visions, views, values, feelings, ideas, and experiences. Accept and acknowledge these unique views.
- Identify associated fears and desires. Give voice to your views, feelings, and experiences. (An example of a unique issue is Arthur Jay's fear of being stereotyped as a "ruthless American" or a "gutless wimp." His acknowledgement helped his group to address private fears publicly.)

The Karmic Change Method and Scripts in Our Heads in Chapter Seven are useful in identifying uniqueness.

Step 4. Transform the Unique into Universal Resources

In this step, the unique views, experiences, voices, and visions of individuals are valued as the ingredients for creating universal resources. Once in place, the resources will be used to enhance individual uniqueness. In other words, take the unique from individuals and transform it into resources to be used communally. By working with the unique, the group will learn to identify what is universal (Allen, 1994, 1996b). For example, AJ's leadership inertia in the composite company TCom seems, at first glance, like a personal weakness. Upon exploration, it becomes obvious that the impasse is part of a universal pattern in leadership development. AJ's personal (unique) process of awakening becomes a guide for overcoming inertia for his whole team (universal). The following are some guidelines for completing Step 4, along with some examples.

- List unique issues (AJ's leadership inertia).

- Identify in what way each issue is unique (fear of being labeled as a ruthless American or gutless wimp).

- Identify the universal significance of the uniqueness (stereotyping and fear of being stereotyped).

- Collect personal experiences relating to the unique issue in question (AJ invites others to share experiences related to stereotyping).

- Conduct community research relating to the unique issue (AJ asks Julee to conduct a survey on stereotyping. The survey indicates stereotyping is quite widespread in TCom and Linco).

- Design prototype products, services, or processes (AJ requests help from the practitioners, who adapt Scripts in Our Heads into "Dialogue on Eliminating Stereotypes" [DOES]).

- Test prototypes in the community (AJ tests DOES with his managers).

- Evaluate and adjust the products (AJ broadens his focus to include stereotyping related to race, national origin, gender, age, sexual orientation, occupation, tenure, and other differences).

- Train others to use the products (AJ asks the four practitioners to train his employees to use DOES).

- Spread the use of products to the broader community (DOES is made available to TCom and Linco).

In the foregoing, we have looked at the key steps of the Circles Process method. Exhibit 10.1 is a worksheet for using the method.

Exhibit 10.1. Circles Process Worksheet

System Under Focus: _____

1. **Include Diversity.** What strategies will you use to increase diversity in your system? What strategies will you use to include the diversity in your system?

2. **Create Common Ground.** What can serve as a common ground in your system? How will you care for the common ground in your system?

3. **Identify the Unique.** What are some unique views, experiences, voices and visions in your system?

Exhibit 10.1. Circles Process Worksheet, Cont'd

4. **Transform the Unique into Universal Resources.** Select a unique feature identified in Step 3 and complete the following steps, if appropriate.

   List unique issues:

   Identify in what way each issue is unique:

   Identify the universal significance of the uniqueness:

   Collect personal experiences relating to the unique issue in question:

   Conduct community research relating to the unique issue:

   Design prototype products, services, or processes:

   Test prototypes in the community:

   Evaluate and adjust the products:

   Train others to use the products:

   Spread the use of products to the broader community:

Following are some further thoughts to enhance your understanding of the significance of circles. The list is useful when given to participants at team-building and community-building sessions.

Circles Work

- A circle creates community naturally.
- A circle of people includes everyone.
- A circle has an open space in the middle.
- Everyone in a circle can contribute to and draw gifts from the open space.
- Everyone has a place in the circle.
- We can move in unison in a circle.
- We can move in and out of a circle.
- A circle is a symbol of perfection.
- People from different backgrounds can form circles.
- People from similar backgrounds can form circles.
- Standing in a circle, we harmonize our disparate energies.
- We each bring a unique presence to the circle.
- We share common ground in a circle.
- A circle is easily formed—just come together and leave a common open space in the middle.
- The open space in the center of the circle signifies the potential we can create together.
- The open space in the center of the circle represents the synergy of our differences.
- We can see everyone in a circle.
- Create an opening circle at the start of your work. Create a closing circle when you finish.
- We can link our circle with other circles.
- A circle is complete in itself.

- A circle can grow to include newcomers.

- A circle is a symbol of change and continuity.

Based on the Circles Process, I have created three easy-to-use techniques that I call Opening Circles, Diversity Circles, and Synergy in Community, all of which can be used to facilitate community.

Opening Circles

Opening Circles is an activity for turning a transitory group into a transitory community. Invite all participants to form a large circle. Explain the purpose of the activity. The following is a script you can adapt to meet your purposes:

"You are gathered here to achieve an important purpose. Your time is valuable. To help create the most productive community, I invite you to participate in a sequence of brief activities so as to harmonize your energies.

"You have formed a circle that is a symbol for community. Notice that, although you may not know all the people, you can form a community very easily. This circle is formed through the unique presence of each one of you. Please observe and imagine the open space in the middle. This open space holds the rich diversity you all bring to the circle. This circle is inclusive, because when a newcomer arrives, all you need to do is to shift a little to open up space to include the unique presence of the newcomer. Inclusion is easy.

"Now close your eyes or simply stay silent. Meditate on this new community. Center in yourself and enjoy the connections around you.

"We will energize the circle by doing four things in turn around the circle: (1) Say your name, (2) Tell one thing about yourself that others cannot tell by looking at you (Fielding Institute workshop, 1991), (3) Name one gift or talent you bring to this circle, and (4) Name one gift or talent that you would like to take from this circle."

To ensure the activity is done quickly, model the script as follows: "My name is [Rebecca]. One thing you may not be able to tell by looking at me is [I have a daughter much taller than I am]. A gift that I bring to the circle is [enthusiasm]. A gift I'd like to take back is [trust]."

Tip: This activity can be used with small and large groups. By modeling quick pacing, it can be completed in fifteen minutes with a group of forty.

Diversity Circles

Diversity Circles is a set of movements that explore differences and similarities within a circle. It is an activity for surfacing diversity in community building. I adapted this tool from Marcella Benson-Quaziena's (Allen, Benson-Quaziena, Dawson, Feliz, Lejuste, & Veroff, 1994) structural inequality exercise.

The following script can be adapted for your purposes:

"Form a circle. In this activity, you will get to know some of the similarities and differences within the group. I am going to read some statements aloud and ask you to take a step forward, back, to the left, or to the right if you agree with the statement."

Sample Statements

- Take a step forward if you are interested in learning/leadership/whole system change (and so on).

- Take a step backward if you work in the corporate/nonprofit/public/ private sector.

- Take a step to the right if you have experienced racism/sexism/homo- phobia/discrimination/stereotyping.

- Take a step to the left if you have led an organization change process/developed an enterprise/downsized an operation.

Participants can run the circles themselves. If so, encourage participants to make up statements that are related to the purpose of your learning and the community you are trying to create. The purpose of having people move in a circle is to manifest the diverse energies and experiences within the group. For example, some people may move a lot, some may move only once, and others may not move at all. With every statement, the movements will create a different group pattern. Invite participants to observe the patterns and their own positions within the patterns. To hold the group energy, limit the moves to five or six. Debrief the activity by inviting participants to talk about their experiences and observations.

Tips: Diversity Circles can be used as an introductory exploration of diversity, following the Open Circles exercise. The activity can also be used separately. Questions such as "Have you experienced racism/sexism in this organization?" can help a group acknowledge difficult-to-talk-about issues. Make it a ground rule that participants have the option of passing by staying put. Provide adequate debriefing time after the activity.

In Chapter Nine, you learned about TCom's Synergy Symposium with one of its offshore companies. As a result of that experience, TCom decided to institute a series of organization-wide community conferences. Entitled "Synergy in Community," these conferences promote innovation and partnership.

▶ Application: Synergy in Community

Practitioners Julee, Daryn, Arente, and Hingram used the four actions of the Circles Process to assist TCom in coordinating the conferences. To maximize exchanges from different time zones and geographical locations, the conferences were designed to encourage both synchronous (simultaneous) and asynchronous (at different times) participation. A variety of technology-enabled conferencing methods, such as video-conferencing, electronic caucusing, and webcasting were used to facilitate learning, exchange, and synergy dialogues within the TCom community. The use of technology was also complemented by community practices such as Opening Circles and Diversity Circles. Arthur Jay and the practitioners used Journey Mapping as a frame to help the community track its retrospective, prospective, and continuum change journeys (see Chapter Four). Following are highlights from TCom's Synergy in Community process.

Include Diversity. The effort to include diverse stakeholders—support staff, local community partners, and affiliates from the parent company, Linco—paid off. TCom developed an expanded sense of itself and its many untapped possibilities. The inclusion of diverse voices enabled TCom to learn more about patterns and dragons that immobilized and distracted energies.

Create Common Ground. The use of Journey Mapping and the Synergy Steps helped diverse TCom stakeholders to find common ground. The affirmation of commonality enabled stakeholders to work toward shared goals. The TCom stakeholders decided to de-center TCom management as the controlling center of their community and re-center the community on its collective shared visions and goals (see Chapter Three).

Identify the Unique. The affirmation of commonality created a foundation for TCom to explore and celebrate differences and uniquenesses. The company's traditional corporate culture had taught the management team and employees to be suspicious of differences, fearing that exploring diversity would open a can of worms. The Diversity Systems Matrix (Chapter Five) and the Synergy Steps (Chapter Nine) showed them that diversity could facilitate innovation and transformation.

Transform the Unique into the Universal. Participants were encouraged by the realization that uniqueness could be the raw ingredients for creating universal resources for the whole community. For example, several TCom offshore operations struggled with difficult relationships with local communities. Stakeholders from the local communities also aired their frustration about insensitivity, disrespect, and disregard for collaboration. Through the conferences, the offshore operators and local representatives learned to transform their gripes and complaints into useful guidelines about collaboration (Mink, Mink, & Owen, 1992). They also learned that, instead of viewing each other as barriers, they could work as partners to create better alternatives. ◀

In the foregoing, we discussed several community-building methods based on timeless mythological insights. In this last section, I will highlight the socio-historical dimension in transformation to remind us that change work impacts real people in real time. Sacred Canopy, a method I adapted from sociological research (Driedger, 1996), fits well for this purpose. It serves as a reminder to connect change with human impact.

Sacred Canopies*

The Jewish sacred canopy is a protective, tent-like structure made out of a large blanket, held aloft by four long stakes, one at each corner (see Figure 10.2). Sociologists Peter Berger (1967) and Leo Driedger (1996) refer to the sacred canopy in discussions of sacred reality, community building, and maintenance of religious and ethnic groups. Here, the sacred canopy is a metaphor for whatever provides a group with a sense of order, meaning, and community in the face of surrounding disorder and uncertainty. The following are key elements of the sacred canopy metaphor.

The Protective Roof. This represents a group's desired reality—meaning, order, connections, prosperity, and so on.

The Supporting Stakes. These hold up the roof to create space for the community. The stakes can include culture, language, land, history, ideology, market, and technology. For many groups, religion, language, and culture are important stakes that hold their communities together (Driedger, 1996). For others, such as start-up companies, the stakes may be a vision, a product, a technology, or financing.

The Site. The space that anchors the sacred canopy, the site can be permanent or temporary. For some groups, a geographical homeland is an essential community-building component. For others, the site may be a plot of land or it may be cyberspace.

The Outside. This is the environment that envelops the sacred canopy. The outside can be a hostile environment full of danger, persecution, and discrimination. The outside can also be a land of vital resources.

---

*The material in this section sourced to Leo Driedger was adapted from *Multi-Ethnic Canada: Identities and Inequalities* by Leo Driedger. Copyright © 1996 by Oxford University Press Canada. Adapted by permission of Oxford University Press Canada.

*The term "sacred canopy" is from Peter L. Berger's book, *The Sacred Canopy: Elements of a Sociological Theory of Religion.* It is used here with the permission of the publisher, Doubleday.

Figure 10.2. The Sacred Canopy

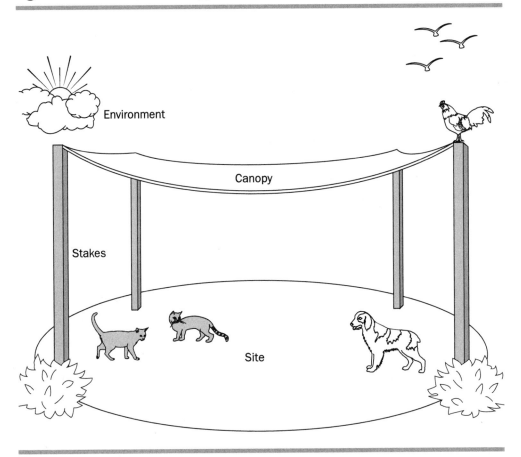

Adapted from *The Sacred Canopy* by P. Berger (1967) and *Multi-Ethnic Canada* by L Driedger (1996).

Driedger (1996) identified three common patterns of sacred canopy in community building: reconstruction, transferral, and transformation.

Reconstruction. This is the process of rebuilding a new sacred canopy to replace a collapsed one. An example is the aboriginal Blackfoot people, who are rebuilding a way of life ruined by colonization (Driedger, 1996). A sacred canopy can also be destroyed by war, natural or industrial disaster, economic revolution, financial mismanagement, loss of market, critical illness, or job loss. Use this pattern to help you identify what has been destroyed in your group's sacred canopy.

Transferral. This involves picking up the supporting stakes and folding up the sacred canopy to re-camp in another location. An example is the transfer of the Hutterite community from Europe to the United States and Canada (Driedger, 1996). The new location can be a country, region, market, or industry. The emphasis here is that few changes are made to the canopy except for the location. Use this pattern to help you identify the best site for the group's sacred canopy.

Transformation. This means adapting the traditional features of a sacred canopy to meet emergent conditions within the community, in the surrounding environment, or in the anchoring site itself. Examples are Jewish, Italian, and Chinese adaptation to life in the United States and Canada (Driedger, 1996). Use this pattern to help you identify what features of a sacred canopy can be adapted to your new circumstances.

Here are some insights deduced from Driedger's studies that can help change agents:

- Rapid and drastic change to the holding stakes of a group's sacred canopy can destroy the entire canopy. Without the protection and support of a meaning-ordering canopy, a group may find it difficult to reconstruct a new way of life.

- Multiple stakes (culture, shared goals, technology, and so on) are required to create and sustain a viable human system.

- Change can devastate a group. Change can also provide opportunities to develop new variations of the holding stakes to support a changing canopy.

Examples of Changing Sacred Canopies

In this section, we'll look at three examples of changing sacred canopies in organizations.

Reconstruction. ZZZbyo is a life science company with a very promising breakthrough discovery. To grow, it seeks and obtains partnership affiliation with a large and well-established firm. ZZZbyo discovers that its partner is using ZZZbyo proprietary research outside the partnership. ZZZbyo files a suit. To focus on the legal battle, ZZZbyo has to shut down all manufacturing. Its stock becomes almost worthless, and 90 percent of the employees have to be let go. The protracted legal case leads to a collapse of ZZZbyo's sacred canopy as the stakes of technology, partnership, financing, and research are destroyed. Only hope sustains ZZZbyo. Eventually, it wins the case and begins reconstructing a new canopy.

Transferral. TradCo was historically a strong mining company. Its sacred canopy is focused on enhancing shareholder value. Its key supporting stakes are management experience, financial savvy, prospecting expertise, and cash reserves. The mining business is viewed as old economy, and the prospects for growth are slim. TradCo decides to use the same business formula that created its past success and apply it to a new line of business. Before long, TradCo finds that the most hospitable site for its sacred canopy is in science and technology. Using its mining perspective and prospecting skills, TradCo soon finds a number of gems among the startups it approaches. One of the resulting acquisitions goes public, and TradCo's investment is multiplied. This story illustrates that, although TradCo changes the industry and economy in which it operates, its sacred canopy remains more or less the same. TradCo simply transfers an effective sacred canopy to a new economic sector and succeeds, at least temporarily.

Transformation. MultiCo is a pipeline company. The stakes holding up MultiCo's sacred canopy are skillful incorporation of technology, an open corporate culture, a penchant for bold moves, and a desire to win. The focus of its sacred canopy is innovation. It likes its line of business and believes it could reinvent itself as a 21st Century company. MultiCo smartly integrates new technologies into its business processes and adapts many e-commerce capabilities. An exciting development is the construction of miles of fiberoptic lines along the rights-of-way of its pipeline tracks. To maximize innovation, MultiCo begins to introduce greater diversity into its workforce. To ensure that the company benefits from the diversity, MultiCo opens up its senior ranks to greater representation of employees from different backgrounds and other parts of the organization. MultiCo begins to change. The desire to win and embrace opportunities continues. But the workforce and the different lines of business are new adaptations. MultiCo effects transformation by simultaneously preserving the old and incorporating the new.

Next, let's look at how to use the Sacred Canopy tool in your own practice.

Sacred Canopy Guidelines

You can use Sacred Canopy with large and small groups, as well as with individuals in re-visioning and community building. Sacred Canopy is an evocative tool. It is especially useful in helping a system to crystallize deeply felt purpose, meaning, and experience in times of threatening change. The questions in Exhibit 10.2 can help you lead the conversations. It is also helpful to show your audience Figure 10.2 to give a visual idea of the concept. Figure 10.2 can also be used as a worksheet to capture your discussion directly on paper.

Exhibit 10.2. Sacred Canopy Worksheet

The Protective Roof

· What kind of sacred canopy does your system have?

· What kind of meaning and experience does the system want to create and preserve in its sacred canopy?

· What can be done to clarify meaning and purpose? What can be done to improve the quality of the experience?

· What can you do to increase cohesiveness?

The Supporting Stakes

· What are the key stakes that hold up the sacred canopy?

· What kind of state are these stakes in?

· What stakes are holding strong?

· What stakes should be replaced? What stakes should be transformed?

· What stakes have been destroyed?

Exhibit 10.2. Sacred Canopy Worksheet, Cont'd

· What stakes are missing? Identify strategies for maintaining the health of the stakes.

The Site

· Describe the anchoring base of your system's sacred canopy.

· Is it the right base?

· How sustainable is it?

· Does your system need to transfer its sacred canopy to a new base?

· If yes, where is this new base? If not, how can you increase the sustainability of the current base?

The Outside

· Describe the quality of the environment outside of your system's sacred canopy.

· What can your system do to make the outer environment more hospitable?

· What alliances can your system forge to increase the quality of the common ground?

Following are some tips on working with the Application Cycle.

Application Cycle Tips
- Application is about passing gifts on to the whole community. This process can be made easier if a system has clarified its own larger purpose.

- Meaning, purpose, and quality of experience can be awkward topics in a corporate setting. Increase the level of comfort by creating conditions for trust and respect.

- The Application Cycle calls for the integration of economic, spiritual, social, and ethical aspects.

- Reflecting on your own needs for such integration can help you become a more empathetic facilitator.

We have looked at the Circles Process and Sacred Canopy methods for facilitating community. You can practice applying them by trying the following activities.

Practice Activities
1. Adapt the Opening Circle or the Diversity Circle for a client group.

2. Draw a picture of your organization as a sacred canopy. Imagine what it will look like in five years.

3. What is your community? What is holding your community together? How do you participate in community?

Summary and Preview

In this chapter, we looked at the challenges of the Application Cycle and the practice of community in the Archetypal Change Journey. We discussed the applications of two methods for community practice: Circles Process and Sacred Canopy. The practice of community can create a sense of belonging among disparate people and transitory organizations. The Sacred Canopy method reminds us that change practice affects real people in real time.

This chapter completes the last Archetypal Change Cycle. As this journey ends, a new cycle will begin. But before you start anew, let's pause and take stock of our travels. In the Epilogue, you will review the challenges and practices of the eight cycles of the Archetypal Change Journey.

Epilogue:
The Gifts of Change

CONGRATULATIONS AND WELCOME to the end of this metaphorical journey. You have completed the eight cycles of the Archetypal Change Journey. In each cycle, you met special challenges. You discovered new perspectives and methods that you can use to tackle those challenges. You became acquainted with the trials and tribulations of our composite companies, TCom, BlissTrek.com, KodeCo, and others. You were introduced to change practitioners Julee, Arente, Daryn, and Hingram and read about their work. You have traveled with Arthur Jay, TCom's CEO, and his colleagues, and you have witnessed some of their successes with organization change.

By completing all eight cycles, you have, in fact, achieved the purpose of the Archetypal Change Journey—expanding awareness and functioning amidst turbulence and complexity. If you think of each change cycle as a circle of awareness and functioning, you will see the circles have expanded with each cycle of change. Figure E1, Circles of Competence, represents this expanding awareness and functioning. By incorporating these cycles and practices into your change work, you can become more adept in guiding change journeys.

Figure E.1. Circles of Competence

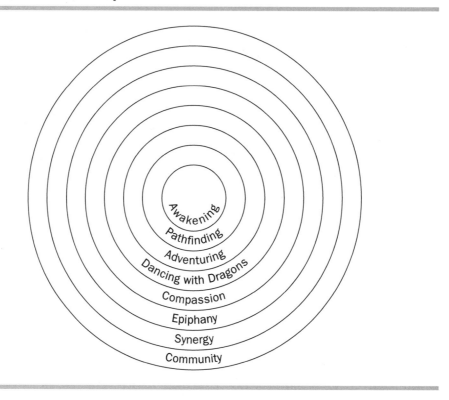

In this book, I addressed the challenge of guiding organization change journeys in interesting times. I have presented the Archetypal Change Journey as one approach to guiding transformation in organizations. My key assumptions are that people and organizations are Archetypal Change Systems (ACS) that can self-organize their own transformation by tapping into change intelligence and energies within and outside their environment. Change agents can enhance their practice by connecting with change intelligence and energies within, and in the burgeoning global human systems around them. I call these assumptions my working Archetypal Change Theory (ACT). Using this working theory as a guide, I tried, in my perspectives and methods, to create synergy by integrating insights from diverse cultures, mythic traditions, new science, and organization development. I sought an approach to change that integrates diversity and enhances the discovery of common ground. I also showed the intertwining transformation journeys between change agents and their organizations. The insights, methods, and resources I described are those I've found helpful in my own turbulent change situations, both professional and personal. They are gifts from my own journey of cultural epiphanies. I hope they will prove useful to you.

Our journey began with the desire to integrate arrow and spiral cultural approaches and to link Eastern and Western ideas about change. The initial effort to establish a synergistic perspective to change permeates the whole of this book. Turbulence and complexity in our growing multicultural systems was the *call* to quest for new ways of thinking and facilitating change. In setting out on this quest, I chose to follow the eight cycles of an Archetypal Change Journey. These change cycles have endured across times and cultures. Each of the eight cycles invites the questing change agent to meet challenges with new practices. Each cycle brings its own gifts of change. These gifts include the epiphanies of radiance, rapture, and bliss, as well as other practical methods and techniques. By accepting the gifts of change, you can guide yourself and your organizations over ever-changing frontiers with anticipation and confidence. Table E.1 summarizes the cycles, challenges, practices, and methods of change.

Table E.1. The Gifts of Change

Cycles	Challenges	Practices	Methods
Inertia	Stagnation, incubation, quandary, revelation	Awakening: Watch for call signals, reconnect with past creativity, discover self-organizing patterns, show other worlds, practice appreciative attention, improvise	De-centering, re-centering, Worlds at Work
Call	Accidental encounter, change in direction, mistakes and mishaps, answer the call	Pathfinding: Create a map, find an orienting device, clarify change intention, choose an effective route	Retrospective, Prospective, and Continuum Journey Mapping

Table E.1. The Gifts of Change, Cont'd

Cycles	Challenges	Practices	Methods
Jump	No return, dangerous opportunity, uncertainty, adventures	Adventuring: Provide perspective, embrace uncertainty, detach from prejudice, explore risk tolerance, trust	Diversity Systems Matrix
Trials	Chaordic energies, multiple tests and stresses, extreme emotions, pull back from change	Dancing with Dragons: Recognize archetypal forms, name the dragon fears, name the dragon desires, walk between fears and desires	Lotus Path, Dragon Quiz, Integrating the Dragons, Down the Pit, Dragon Check-Up Chart
Dissolution	Negative perceptions, turning point, suffering	Compassion: Be open to en-lightenment and transcendence, offer empathetic presence, provide guidance and instruction, coun-tenance suffering	Karmic Change Method, Scripts in Our Heads
Discovery	Clarity and light, the inconceivable is real, experience of epiphanies	Epiphany: Convert power energy into inner light, convert relational energy into rapturous collaboration, convert consuming energy into blissful pursuits	Lotus Path, Three Turns of Transformation

Table E.1. The Gifts of Change, Cont'd

Cycles	Challenges	Practices	Methods
Integration	Incorporate discoveries, reconcile differences, sustain emergent system, create a new vision	Synergy: Attract solitudes, create common ground, accentuate distinctiveness, dissolve boundaries, proliferate resources, journey to the unknown, create new possibilities	Seven Synergy Steps, Synergy Dialogues, Synergy Symposium
Application	Face skepticism and indifference, recognize universal worth, convert insights into practice, get support, adapt to diversity, exercise freedom	Community: Use open process, create shared culture, create anchors, put diversity to work, foster responsible freedom, co-create heritage, enhance mutual renewal	Circles Process: Opening Circles, Diversity Circles, Synergy in Community; Sacred Canopy

I have enjoyed this writing journey. My experiences have been mostly joyous. Some moments were arduous. I spent days stuck in *inertia*. *Call* took me to a bifurcation point—I was in conflict over a choice of paths. At *jump,* I was hesitant: I called the practice associated with *jump* "commitment" and later changed it to "adventuring." In *trials,* I was so fearful of not having enough tools that I created too many and had to cut back. I approached *dissolution* with a saddened attitude, but ended up hopeful and excited about the idea of a positive reincarnation. *Discovery* was a joy. I loved the practice of epiphany. *Integration* was difficult because I had so much material for the topic. Finally, in *application,* I paused long, trying to link different ideas into a whole. Through this journey, I learned that just beyond terror and turbulence, there is a center that is always still and unchanging.

I hope our journey together has been worthwhile. This book is a beginning step in applying cultural synergy and mythic power in organization transformation. To further this journey, I hope you will feel free to tinker and improvise with the insights, methods, and tools to make them fit your needs. I welcome dialogue, debate, critique, and collaboration. I am eager to hear about your journeys and change stories. I invite you to visit our website at www.culturalsynergy.com. May bliss follow you in all your adventures.

References

Ackerman Anderson, L., & Anderson, D. (2001). *The change leader's roadmap.* San Francisco, CA: Jossey-Bass/Pfeiffer.

Adler, N.J. (1980). Cultural synergy: The management of cross-cultural organizations. In W.W. Burke & L.D. Goodstein (Eds.), *Trends and issues in OD: Current theory and practice* (pp. 163–184). San Francisco, CA: Jossey-Bass/Pfeiffer.

Adler, N.J. (1995). Competitive frontiers: Cross-cultural management and the 21st century. *International Journal of Intercultural Relations, 19*(4), 523–537.

Adler, N.J., & Bird, F. (1988). International dimensions of executive integrity: Who is responsible for the world? In S. Srivastva and Associates (Eds.), *Executive integrity: The search for executive values in organizational life* (pp. 243–337). San Francisco, CA: Jossey-Bass.

Albrecht, L., & Brewer, R.M. (1990). *Bridges of power: Women's multicultural alliances.* Santa Cruz, CA: New Society Publishers.

Allee, V. (2000). Knowledge networks and communities of practice. *OD Practitioner, 32*(4), 4–12.

Allen, R.C. (1991). Opening the closed off. *Organization Development Network conference proceedings* (pp. 9–12). Portland, OR: OD Network.

Allen, R.C. (1994). *The circles project.* Unpublished report. Calgary, Alberta, Canada: Delta Learning Organization.

Allen, R.C. (1995a). *Discovery of an embodying self: Cancer, identities, narratives.* Unpublished doctoral dissertation. Santa Barbara, CA: Fielding Institute.

Allen, R.C. (1995b). Navigating change in chaotic times: Insights from five archetypal journeys. *Organization Development Network conference proceedings* (pp. 285–289). South Orange, NJ: OD Network.

Allen, R.C. (1996a). Joyous connections: The great archetypal renewal cycle. *Organization Development Network conference proceedings* (pp. 48–52). South Orange, NJ: OD Network.

Allen, R.C. (1996b). Networks, circles, & common ground. Unpublished paper. Calgary, Alberta, Canada: Delta Learning Organization.

Allen, R.C. (1997). Confucius and tao: Playing with paradox. *Organization Development Network conference proceedings* (pp. 64–68). South Orange, NJ: OD Network.

Allen, R.C. (1999). Sociology of Canadian society. In S. Murray & R.C. Allen, *Canadian society and the contemporary world.* Vancouver, BC: Certified General Accountants of Canada and University of Calgary.

Allen, R.C. (2000). Archetypal magic and systems transformation. *OD Practitioner, 32*(4), 49–55.

Allen, R.C., Benson-Quaziena, M., Dawson, P., Feliz, E., Lejuste, C., & Veroff, S. (1994). *Women of color and white women coming together.* Workshop at Organization Development Network Annual Conference, Baltimore, MD, USA.

Anonymous South Asian Sages. (1999). *The Upanishads.* (E. Easwaran, trans.). Tomales, CA: Nilgiri Press. (Originally published in the 8th and 4th Centuries BCE and 16th Century CE.)

Arrien, A. (Ed.)(1998). *Working together: Producing synergy by honoring diversity.* Pleasanton, CA: New Leaders Press.

Bellman, G. (1990). *The consultant's calling: Bringing who you are to what you do.* San Francisco, CA: Jossey-Bass.

Berger, P. (1967). *The sacred canopy: Elements of a sociological theory of religion.* Garden City, NY: Doubleday.

Bohm, D. (1980). *Wholeness and the implicate order.* London, England: Ark Paperbacks.

Briggs, J., & Peat, F. (1990). *Turbulent mirror: An illustrated guide to chaos theory and the science of wholeness.* New York: Harper & Row.

Buchmann, M. (1989). *The script of life in modern society: Entry into adulthood in a changing world.* Chicago, IL: University of Chicago Press.

Bunker, B.B., & Alban, B. (1996). Principles and practice of large group interventions. *Organization Development Network conference proceedings* (pp. 53–56). South Orange, NJ: OD Network.

Bunyan, J. (1922). *The pilgrim's progress.* London, England: Robert Culley. (Originally published in 1678.)

Burke, W.W. (1987). *Organization development: A normative view.* Reading, MA: Addison-Wesley.

Campbell, J. (1968). *The hero with a thousand faces.* Princeton, NJ: Princeton University Press. (Originally published in 1949.)

Campbell, J. (1986). *The inner reaches of outer space: Metaphor as myth and as religion.* New York: Alfred van der Marck/Harper & Row.

Campbell, J. (1989). *The world of Joseph Campbell: Transformations of myth through time.* A production of William Free Productions, Mythology Limited, and Holoform Research Inc. Chicago, IL: Public Media Video.

Campbell, J. (1990). *Transformations of myth through time.* New York: Harper & Row.

Campbell, J. (1993). *Myths to live by.* London, England: Penguin Arkana.

Campbell, J., with Moyers, B. (1988). *The power of myth* [PBS television Series]. Apostrophe S Productions. New York: Mystic Fire Video Inc.

Campbell, J., & Moyers, B. (1991). *The power of myth.* New York: Anchor Books.

Capra, F. (1982). *The turning point: Science, society, and the rising culture.* Toronto, ON: Bantam.

Chopra, D. (1990). *Quantum healing: Exploring the frontiers of mind/body medicine.* New York: Bantam.

Chopra, D. (1994). *The seven spiritual laws of success: A practical guide to the fulfillment of your dreams.* San Rafael, CA: Amber-Allen.

Collier, R. (1926). *The secret of the ages.* New York: Author.

Cooper, D.A. (1992*). Silence, simplicity and solitude: A guide for spiritual retreat.* New York: Bell Tower.

Cross, E.Y., Katz, J.H, Miller, F.A., & Seashore, E.W. (1994). *The promise of diversity: Over 40 voices discuss strategies for eliminating discrimination in organizations.* Alexandria, VA: NTL Institute/New York: Irwin.

Curran, K.M., Seashore, C.N., & Welp, M.G. (1995). Use of self as an instrument of change. *Organization Development Network conference proceedings* (pp. 115–119). South Orange, NJ: OD Network.

Downing, C. (1990). Masks of goddess: A feminist response. In D.C. Noel (Ed.), *Paths to the power of myth: Joseph Campbell and the study of religion* (pp. 97–107). New York: Crossroad.

Driedger, L. (1996). *Multi-ethnic Canada: Identities and inequalities.* Toronto, ON: Oxford University Press.

Eliot, T.S. (1986). The waste land. In M.H. Abrams (Ed.), *The Norton anthology of English literature* (5th ed.), Vol. 2 (pp. 2181–2196). New York: W.W. Norton. (Originally published in 1922.)

Fielding Institute Contract Admission Workshop. (1991, September). Santa Barbara, California.

Ford, C.W. (1999). *The hero with an African face: Mythic wisdom of traditional Africa.* New York: Bantam.

Fuller, B. (2000). *Glossary.* Buckminster Fuller Institute. [*www.bfi.org/SynEinstein.htm*].

Gilligan, C. (1982). *In a different voice: Psychological theory and women's development.* Cambridge, MA: Harvard University Press.

Helmstetter, S. (1987). *What to say when you talk to yourself.* New York: Pocket.

Hock, D. (1998). *An epidemic of institutional failure: Organizational development and the new millenium* [Keynote Address]. Organization Development Network Annual Conference, New Orleans, Louisiana, USA.

Holmes, E. (1988). *The science of mind.* New York: G.P. Putnam's Sons. (Originally published in 1926.)

Jung, C.G. (1969). Approaching the unconscious. In C.G. Jung, M.-L. von Franz, J.L. Henderson, J. Jacobi, & A. Jaffe (Eds.), *Man and his symbols.* Garden City, NY: Doubleday.

Lao Zi. (1998). *The works of Lao Zi: Truth and nature* (popularly know as Dao-de-jing [L. Cheng, trans.]). Taipei, Taiwan: The World Book Company, Ltd. (Originally published ca. 500–ca.220 BCE.)

Librizzi, C.G., & Cadario, P. (2000) A diversity approach to global teams. *OD Practitioner, 32*(4), 37–41.

Marshak, R.J. (1993a). Lewin meets Confucius: A re-view of the OD model of change. *Journal of Applied Behavioral Science, 29*(4), 393–415.

Marshak, R.J. (1993b). Managing the metaphors of change. *Organizational Dynamics, 22*(1), 44–56.

Marshak, R.J. (1993c). Training and consulting in Korea. *OD Practitioner, 25*(2), 16–21.

Maslow, A. (1973). *The farther reaches of human nature.* New York: Penguin.

Maturana, H.R., & Varela, F.J. (1992). *The tree of knowledge: The biological roots of human understanding.* Boston, MA: Shambhala.

McManus, K.L. (1994). Ethnography and the new science: The utility of Jungian-based analysis and local intervention in the transformation of large systems. *Organization Development Network conference proceedings* (pp. 173–178). Portland, OR: OD Network.

McMurdy, D. (2000, November) The human cost of mergers. *Maclean's,* p. 128.

McWhinney, W. (1990). How do you pick a path of change? Old myths create new realities. *Organization Development Network conference proceedings* (pp. 189–194). Portland, OR: OD Network.

McWhinney, W. (1992). *Paths of change: Strategic choices for organizations and society.* Thousand Oaks, CA: Sage.

Mink, O.G., Mink, B.P., & Owen, K.Q. (1992). *Groups at work.* Englewood Cliffs, NJ: Educational Technology Publications.

Morgan, G. (1986). *Images of organizations.* Thousand Oaks, CA: Sage.

Nichols, E. (1991). *People of color day* [Keynote Address]. Organization Development Network Annual Conference, Long Beach, California, USA.

Noel, D.C. (Ed.). (1990). *Paths to the power of myth: Joseph Campbell and the study of religion.* New York: Crossroad.

Olson, E., & Eoyang, G. (2001). *Facilitating organization change: Lessons from complexity science.* San Francisco, CA: Jossey-Bass/Pfeiffer.

Osbon, D.K. (1991). *Reflections on the art of living: A Joseph Campbell companion.* New York: HarperPerennial.

Owen, H. (1997). *Open space technology: A user's guide.* San Francisco, CA: Berrett-Koehler.

Peat, D. (1991). *The philosopher's stone: Chaos, synchronicity, and the hidden order of the world.* New York: Bantam.

Platt, D. (1999). *Mysticism in world religions.* [*www.digiserve.com/Muslim/index.html*].

Prigogine, I., & Stengers, I. (1984). *Order out of chaos: Man's new dialogue with nature.* Toronto, ON: Bantam.

Renwick, G. (1986). *Workshop on intercultural training.* Stanford Institute of Intercultural Communication. Palo Alto, California, USA.

Sambhava, P. (ca.717–ca.762 CE.)(1994). *The Tibetan book of the dead: Liberation through understanding in the between.* (Composed by Padama Sambhava; discovered by Karma Lingpa; R.A.F. Thurman, trans.). New York: Bantam. (Originally published in the 14th Century CE.)

Schein, E.H., & Beckhard, R. (1987). Foreword. In W.W. Burke, *Organization development: A normative view.* Reading, MA: Addison-Wesley.

Senge, P.M. (1990). *The fifth discipline: The art and practice of the learning organization.* New York: Doubleday Currency.

Taylor, C.H., & Finley, P. (1997). *Images of the journey in Dante's divine comedy.* New Haven, CT: Yale University Press.

Tobin, R. (1999). Beyond borders: International organization development. *Organization Development Network conference proceedings* (pp. 64–69). South Orange, NJ: OD Network.

von Franz, M.-L. (1969). Conclusion: Science and the unconscious. In C.G. Jung, M.-L. Franz, J.L. Henderson, J. Jacobi, & A. Jaffe (Eds.), *Man and his symbols* (pp.304–310). Garden City, NY: Doubleday.

Watkins, J.M., & Mohr, B. (2001). *Appreciative inquiry: Change at the speed of imagination.* San Francisco, CA: Jossey-Bass/Pfeiffer.

Weisbord, M.R., & Janoff, S. (1995). *Future search: An action guide to finding common ground in organizations and communities.* San Francisco, CA: Berrett-Koehler.

Wheatley, M.J. (1994). *Leadership and the new science: Learning about organization from an orderly universe.* San Francisco, CA: Berrett-Koehler.

Wilson, D. (1979). *Total mind power: How to use the other 90% of your mind.* New York: Berkley Books.

Wolinsky, S. (1993). *Quantum consciousness: The guide to experiencing quantum psychology.* Norfolk, CT: Bramble Books.

Wu, C.E. (ca.1500–ca.1582) (1984). *The journey to the west* (A.C. Yu, trans.). Chicago, IL: University of Chicago Press. (Originally published in the 16th Century.)

Zukav, G. (1980). *The dancing wu li masters: An overview of the new physics.* New York: Bantam.

About the Author

Rebecca Chan Allen, president of Delta Learning Organization, is a facilitator in cultural synergy and creative transformation. Her practice integrates insights and methods from different disciplines and cultural traditions. Her clients include HRD Canada, Imperial Oil, ScotiaBank, Amoco, Exxon, Shell, CP Rail, AEC International, Nortel, PanCanadian, YMCA, YWCA, and others.

Dr. Chan Allen has a doctorate in human and organization systems, master's degrees in organization development and in sociology, and a bachelor's degree in economics. She is a professional member of the NTL Institute for Applied Behavioral Science. She has taught university courses, coordinated a multicultural training institute and multilingual social services, and operated an arts business.

Dr. Chan Allen was selected for *Training's New Guard 2001* by the American Society for Training and Development (ASTD), was the World Bank lecturer at Keio

University in Tokyo in 1998, and, in 1991, was nominated for the Calgary YWCA Women of Distinction and HR Canada's Practitioner of the Year.

Born in China, Dr. Chan Allen has lived, studied, and worked in Asia, Europe, the United States, and Canada. She lives in Calgary, Alberta, and Vancouver, British Columbia.

About the Editors

William J. Rothwell, Ph.D., is professor of human resource development in the College of Education at The Pennsylvania State University, University Park. He is also president of Rothwell and Associates, a private consulting firm that specializes in a broad array of organization development, human resource development, performance consulting, and human resource management services.

Dr. Rothwell has authored, co-authored, edited, or co-edited numerous publications, including *Practicing Organization Development* (with R. Sullivan and G. McLean, Jossey-Bass/Pfeiffer, 1995). Dr. Rothwell's latest publications include *The ASTD Reference Guide to Workplace Learning and Performance*, 3rd ed., 2 vols. (with H. Sredi, HRD Press, 2000); *The Competency Toolkit*, 2 vols. (with D. Dubois, HRD Press, 2000); *Human Performance Improvement: Building Practitioner Competence* (with C. Hohne and S. King, Gulf Publishing, 2000); *The Complete Guide to Training Delivery: A Competency-Based*

Approach (with S. King and M. King, Amacom, 2000); *Building In-House Leadership and Management Development Programs* (with H. Kazanas, Quorum Books, 1999); *The Action Learning Guidebook* (Jossey-Bass/Pfeiffer, 1999); and *Mastering the Instructional Design Process,* 2nd ed. (with H. Kazanas, Jossey-Bass/Pfeiffer, 1998).

Dr. Rothwell's consulting client list includes thirty-two companies from the *Fortune* 500.

Roland **Sullivan** has worked as an organization development (OD) pioneer with nearly eight hundred organizations in ten countries and virtually every major industry.

Mr. Sullivan specializes in the science and art of systematic and systemic change, executive team building, and facilitating Whole System Transformation Conferences—large interactive meetings with from three hundred to fifteen hundred people.

Mr. Sullivan has taught courses in OD at seven universities, and his writings on OD have been widely published. With Dr. Rothwell and Dr. McLean, he was co-editor of *Practicing OD: A Consultant's Guide* (Jossey-Bass/Pfeiffer, 1995).

For over two decades, Mr. Sullivan has served as chair of the OD Institute's Committee to Define Knowledge and Skills for Competence in OD and was a recent recipient of the Outstanding OD Consultant of the World award from the OD Institute.

Mr. Sullivan's current professional learning is available at *www.RolandSullivan.com.*

Kristine **Quade** is an independent consultant who combines her background as an attorney with a master's degree in organization development from Pepperdine University, and years of experience as both an internal and external OD consultant.

Ms. Quade draws from experiences in guiding teams from divergent areas within corporations and across many levels of executives and employees. She has facilitated leadership alignment, culture change, support system alignment, quality process improvements, organizational redesign, and the creation of clear strategic intent that results in significant bottom-line results. A believer in whole systems change, she has developed the expertise to facilitate groups ranging in size from eight to two thousand in the same room for a three-day change process.

Recognized as the 1996 Minnesota Organization Development Practitioner of the Year, Ms. Quade teaches in the master's programs at Pepperdine University and the University of Minnesota at Mankato and the master's and doctoral programs at the University of St. Thomas in Minneapolis. She is a frequent presenter at the Organization Development National Conference and also at the International OD Congress and the International Association of Facilitators.

Index

Radiance energy: described, 149; transformation of power into, 156–157, 160
Random Flow Journey Map, 33*f*
Rapture energy, 150
Re-centering technique, 54–55, 56–57*e*
Reconstruction of sacred canopy, 208
Relational dragon, 107–108, 111*e*, 116*e*
Relational energy, 157, 159
Relationship ("guanxi"), 14–15
Ren-Relational Ethics, 182*f*
Repostpective karma, 130–131
Responsible freedom, 194–195
Retrospective journal mapping: described, 71–72*f*; TCom's application of, 7678
Retrospective karma, 129–130
Rumi (Sufi mystic), 64

S

Sacred canopies: described, 207–209; examples of changing, 209–210; guidelines for, 210; illustration of, 208*f*
Sacred Canopy Worksheet, 211*e*–212*e*
Sambhava, P., 123, 124, 125, 174
Sample Synergy Form, 180*e*
Schein, E. H., 13
Scripts in Our Heads: Gilda's application of, 139–141; history of, 122; practice activities for, 145; steps for using, 133–136; TCom application of, 136–139; tips for using, 136, *See also* Karmic Change Method (KCM)
Scripts in Our Heads Worksheet I, 141*e*–142*e*
Scripts in Our Heads Worksheet II, 143*e*–144*e*
Seashore, C. N., 5
Seashore, E. W., 5
Seduction, 108
Self-awareness, 9
Self-organizing: creating "software" for, 127; defining, 9
Senge, P., 22
Seven Energies Assessment Form, 161*e*–162

Seven Synergy Steps: accentuate distinctiveness, 173; AJ's application of, 183–184; attract solitudes, 172; Bjorn and AJ's application of, 178–179; create common ground, 172–173; create new possibilities, 174–175; described, 170, 172; dissolve boundaries, 173; journey into the unknown, 174; listed, 171*f*; proliferate resources, 174
ShenkiCo, 186
Sheung-Ngaw, 84
Smithe, T., 91
Spiral archetype, 8
Spiral Journey Map, 32, 33*f*, 34
Spiral metaphor, 15–16*t*
Star Wars (movie series), 12
Stengers, I., 123
Stereotype anatomy, 135*f*
Structural landscape of organization: described, 93*f*; instructional script for using, 94; KodeCo's application of, 98; Linco's application of, 96; worksheet for using, 95*e*
Supporting canopy stakes, 207
Symbolic culture, 93
Synergy: application to community, 205–206; applications of, 178–186; creating, 167–168; defining, 9, 169–170; facilitating, 170; practice activities for, 188; seven steps in, 171–175; tips on increasing capacity of, 188, *See also* Integration Cycle
Synergy dialogues: AJ's experience with, 182–184; Bjorn and AJ experience with, 178–179; blank, 181*e*
Synergy Form, 180*e*
Synergy Quiz, 175*e*–177*e*
Synergy symposium: application of, 184–185; facilitating a, 185; ShenkiCo and TCom's, 186
Synergy Worksheet, 187*e*
Systemic landscape of organization: described, 93; instructional script for using, 95; KodeCo's application of, 98; Linco's application of, 97; worksheet for using, 95*e*
Systems thinking archetypes, 22–23